HANDBOOK FOR HANDGUNS

A Practical Guide to Ownership, Selection & Use

July 2014

Charles Bruckerhoff

A Publication of Foresight

All Rights Reserved
Copyright © 2014

ISBN: 978-0-9905838-5-1

For information address:

Foresight, A Division of Curriculum Research & Evaluation, Inc.
237 Singleton Road
Chaplin, CT 06235-2223

Phone: 860-455-1229

Handbook for Handguns is available in iBook, Kindle and paperback versions.

Email: info@ForesightForGoodGuys.com

Web site/homepage: http://www.ForesightForGoodGuys.com

First Edition
Published in the United States of America

Image of the Declaration of Independence used with permission from Seth Kaller, Inc.

No part of this publication may be reproduced in any form whatsoever, by photograph, digital copy or transfer, fax transmission or any other mechanical or electronic means. Nor can it be broadcast or transmitted by translation into any language, nor by electronic recording or otherwise, without the express written permission from the author—except by a reviewer, who may quote brief passages for critical articles and/or reviews.

DESIGNED BY CHARLES BRUCKERHOFF

12 11 10 9 8 7 6 5 4 3 2 1

Dedication

My sons - Jeffrey, Aaron, Matthew and Michael

My grandchildren - Everett, Ava, Evelyn and Thomas

Foreword

Handbook for Handguns provides an in-depth discussion of handguns to help readers answer these questions: why people choose to own a handgun, how to handle handguns safely and what kind of pistol or revolver to use for different shooting interests. Safe use of handguns is the constant concern.

Handguns are ubiquitous in American society and culture, and possession of a handgun is one of the most controversial topics of our time. Gun ownership is a 2nd Amendment right in the Bill of Rights in the Constitution of the United States of America. A citizen who chooses to exercise that right lawfully should be able to do so without interference, as with all other constitutional rights.

There are individuals and groups that are staunchly against gun ownership by private citizens. The anti-gun movement opposes federal and state laws that favor gun ownership and fights to enact new laws and reinterpret existing laws to restrict or eliminate gun ownership, including repeal of the 2nd Amendment.

Gun rights advocates strive against the anti-gun bias to uphold the 2nd Amendment and to defeat laws that would infringe on an individual's right to possess firearms.

Gun owners are not criminals, they are law-abiding citizens who choose to keep and bear arms in the United States of America.

Criminals do not follow laws. They obtain guns illegally to commit crimes of theft, rape and murder, instilling fear and horror in innocent victims, their families and loved ones.

Most gun owners do not broadcast that they have rifles, shotguns or handguns because it can bring unwelcome attention. They have good, strong personal reasons for owning and using handguns for self-defense, home or business defense, plinking, target shooting, hunting, competitive shooting, collecting, and the 2nd Amendment.

If you choose to own a gun, have an explanation for doing so. Friends, family members, neighbors, and acquaintances will find out that you own a gun and they will ask: "Why do you own a gun?" Often, they are just curious. Most Americans approve of gun ownership although they don't know much about guns or how to use them. For the curious ones, talk it up, because you might win a convert or keep a rational, understanding ally on our side. In some cases, the person who asks why you own a gun may want to pick a fight. For anti-gunners, say why you choose to own a gun. If that's not accepted save your arguments for legislative hearings and court cases in order to protect the 2nd Amendment.

Most of the handguns photographed for *Handbook for Handguns* are from my personal collection. They are not all the latest handguns, although some are recent productions and some are classics. The attempt in this book has been to present representative samples of handguns for different purposes, not the latest products. An attempt to broadcast the most up to date handguns on the market would quickly make a publication, other than a journal, obsolete.

My career path includes a MS and Ph.D. from the University of Wisconsin, undergraduate and graduate level teaching of curriculum development, theory and philosophy of education, and field-based research of disadvantaged youth and innovative educational programs. In 1995, I established the firm, Curriculum Research and Evaluation, Inc. to improve teaching and learning in public and private educational programs.

Work in firearms education includes teaching basic pistol courses and teaching and curriculum development for hunter safety training. Personal interests in the shooting sports includes skeet and trap shooting and sporting clays, quail, woodcock, squirrel and rabbit hunting, big game hunting, competitive pistol, rifle and shotgun shooting, bullet molding, reloading cartridges, Life Member in a local sportsmen's club, NRA Endowment Life Member and gun collecting. As a younger man I served in the 31st Combat Engineer Battalion of the U. S. Army in Vietnam.

Shooting guns is one of many personal interests. I study American history, from the voyages of discovery onward, especially original writings of persons who lived through those times, historians with a respect for facts, truth and accurate storytellers. I visit historical sites, museums and archives to see first-hand the places where events unfolded and to study artifacts of antiquity. I collect books in these areas, especially hard-to-find books written by eyewitnesses, and first editions of American literature, including the naturalists - Emerson, Thoreau, Burroughs, Muir, Leopold and Olson. Classical literatures in America, Europe and Asia from antiquity through modern times, bookbinding worn and pages corner-bent, they fill the shelves of my library. Internet extends my home's research capabilities for unlimited exploration online.

There is always work to be done, but there is also time to pursue hobbies and other personal interests. A day hunting, shooting, hiking or fishing is better than a day on the job.

Family time is the most precious of all.

Several years ago I discovered machine quilting. The first quilt I made was a queen-sized "Buckeye Beauty" for my wife who got a pleasant surprise on Christmas morning. Since then I have made several other quilts for my sons and friends of the family. Quilting, like hunting and shooting, is a passion.

At the start of handgun ownership, concentrate on safety and discover the various self-defense and sporting opportunities for handgun use. Over time, fit handguns into the other pursuits that make up your lifestyle. Gun ownership and use should make sense to you and others; it should not be unexpected or unwelcome to family and friends.

If you live alone, it may be easy to develop an interest in pistols. But usually the place called home includes friends, spouses, children and relatives who either live there permanently or visit from time to time. If you wish to pursue pistol ownership, you should talk about it with your loved ones and prepare them for your new interest. Explain why you wish to obtain a pistol and how it will be stored and used safely. Get the other family members involved in the pistol shooting sports if they are interested. If they are not interested, that's OK. Always give family and friends all the assurances they need that your home will be warm and safe. Store and use firearms correctly - safely - and go to the range regularly to develop your pistol shooting skills. Have fun practicing.

Handbook for Handguns would not be possible if not for colleagues, friends and loved ones. John Postemski is a generous, sincere and hardworking man. He's just over 80 years old and can put men 30 years younger in the shade. Dave Thompson, from the same generation as John P., taught me about black powder firearms and accuracy. Through many years these two guys have given me priceless pointers for life.

Army buddies who covered my back in the worst of times and still today are always prepared: Bob Brooks, Doyle Dietsch, Tom Giese and Greg Jennings; and recently from out of the blue came Bill Bilodeau and Dave Stratton. Tom and Carol Briggs give consultation and friendship, and have done so for years. David Englander, a skillful attorney and gifted teacher, graciously answered the call for help while on a hiking trip in Wales. My neighbor Lenny Patera and his wife Kathy are so thoughtful and generous. And there's Don Bajger the indefatigable past-president of my local sportsman's club.

Getting photographs of scarce ammunition and guns is very difficult in these times. These gun stores graciously offered assistance: Cabela's of East Hartford - especially Phil Orzel, Hoffman's Gun Shop, and Kittery Trading Post. Christie and Jimmy of Hoffman's Gun Shop assisted in the classroom and shooting range. Jim Cummings of Columbia Center Sports provided a choice photo op at his outdoor range. Sean and his golf team at the University Club of Connecticut kindly provided tee off shots under an extremely impressive Southern New England sky. David Oaks gave encouragement in his first class style and also useful commentary. Bill Poole at the NRA tracked down a resource and bumped the whole project up several notches.

Gary Berlin read the manuscript, provided photos and gave very helpful, candid recommendations for its improvement. Jim Moore founded OutdoorRoadmap LLC, a cutting-edge online source for hunter safety training and how-to articles on related topics. Jim has been very encouraging and his company provided helpful resources for this project. Grant Gregory set the hunter education world on fire with his vision and generous support for creating the best-in-class online hunter safety training programs for students and instructors. Working with Grant was the ultimate eye-opener, a distinctive game-changing event.

Over the past twenty-five years hundreds of students in the university courses, and so many others in Basic Pistol and Hunter Safety classes helped me get things right. I am most grateful for their help.

My four wonderful sons, their wives and my grandchildren are a constant source of joy. I love them all dearly. Their exploits are fascinating, to say the least. My brothers and sisters and other family members and friends in the home state keep the fires burning hot. Thanks y'all.

My wife Theresa is my best friend, most articulate and penetrating critic, a loving wife and wonderful mother and grandmother of the children who grace our family. I am forever thankful for her patience, tireless work, thoughtfulness and love.

Chaplin, Connecticut

July 2014

Disclaimer

The author accepts no responsibility for accidents or injuries or any other problem arising from the use of information in this book or any part of this book. The READER should always exercise common sense and caution when handling firearms and in accordance with all applicable laws. Although every effort was made in the preparation of this book to present accurate information in order to help the READER prepare for safe effective use of handguns, the responsibility for using the firearm nevertheless rests solely with the user. Therefore, the author disclaims all possible liability, consequential, incidental, actual or otherwise, for any damages or injuries caused by the use or misuse of the information contained in this book and which is supplied without representation or warranty of any kind. Furthermore, there is no intent in the publication of this book to support or encourage in any way criminal activity or the unlawful killing of animals.

Table of Contents

Dedication	iii
Foreword	v
Disclaimer	ix
The Foundation of Liberty	13
Federal and State Laws	19
A Brief History of Guns	23
Gun Safety Rules	33
Revolvers and Semi-Automatics	45
Ammunition	65
Ballistics	79
Preparing for Live Fire	85
Taking First Shots	97
Cleaning Handguns	107
Storing Handguns	113
Next Steps	119
Glossary	127
Answers to Quiz Questions	139

Chapter 1

The Foundation of Liberty

The United States Constitution established the right of the people to rule and the Bill of Rights secured for the people personal freedoms, limitations on government's power and reservation of some powers to the states and the general public. Over time the United States Supreme Court determines through interpretation of court cases the extent of protection afforded by the Bill of Rights.

United States Constitution

We the people of the United States of America are privileged. We have inherited rights and liberties never before known, here and abroad. People of many other nations today still do not enjoy the freedoms we have. Political freedom is precious and fragile. Our personal control over life, liberty and the pursuit of happiness may be lost unless we continuously require our government and all governing officials to uphold the standards set forth in the documents adopted by the 13 Founding Fathers.

The Continental Congress, made up of representatives of the 13 states of America, adopted by unanimous vote the Declaration of Independence on July 4, 1776. This most famous sentence of the Declaration established the moral standard for the United States of America, the world as our witness: "We hold these truths to be self-evident, that all men are created equal, that they are endowed by their Creator with certain unalienable Rights, that among these are Life, Liberty and the pursuit of Happiness." The American people are endowed by the Creator with "certain unalienable rights," which cannot be taken away and are not granted by government.

The American Revolutionary War for independence from rule by England started earlier on April 19, 1775, at Lexington and Concord, Massachusetts, 15 months before the Declaration, and ended eight years later with the signing of the Treaty of Paris on September 3, 1783. Twenty-five thousand Americans lost their lives in the War of Independence.

On September 17, 1787, the United States Constitution was adopted at the Constitutional Convention in Philadelphia, Pennsylvania. On December 15, 1791, the first ten amendments to the Constitution, known as the Bill of Rights, were adopted. This was the first constitution of its kind in the history of the world: the American people rule themselves. This bold assertion has influenced people of other nations who sought independence from foreign or tyrannical rule.

From the Preamble to the Constitution: "We the People of the United States, in Order to form a more perfect Union, establish Justice, insure domestic Tranquility, provide for the common defense, promote the general Welfare, and secure the Blessings of Liberty to ourselves and our Posterity, do ordain and establish this Constitution for the United States of America."

First Amendment

"Congress shall make no law respecting an establishment of religion, or prohibiting the free exercise thereof; or abridging the freedom of speech, or of the press, or of the right of the people to assemble, and to petition the Government for a redress of grievances."

The First Amendment to the United States Constitution established the five pillars of freedom:

- Speech: people have the right to speak freely without government interference.

- Press: news media outlets have the right to publish news, information and opinions without government interference. Individuals also have the right to publish news, information and opinions.

- Religion: the government shall not establish a religion and shall protect each individual's right to practice or not practice religion without government interference.

- Petition: people have the right to petition the government in favor of or against policies that affect them or about which they feel strongly. Freedom to petition includes the right to collect signatures to support a cause or to lobby Congress for or against legislation.

◎ Assembly: people have the right to come together in public places to march, protest, demonstrate, carry signs and in all manner of non-violent ways express their views. People may join and associate with groups and organizations without government interference.

Although there are restrictions set over time by Supreme Court rulings, the First Amendment to the United States Constitution protects the rights of freedom of religion and freedom of expression from interference by the government.

Second Amendment

"A well regulated militia being necessary to the security of a free state, the right of the people to keep and bear arms shall not be infringed."

The Second Amendment to the United States Constitution protects the right of the individual to keep and bear arms. This right allows the individual to possess and use firearms, with some restrictions, for traditionally lawful purposes, including home defense and self-defense. In *District of Columbia v. Heller*[1], the Supreme Court ruled that the original intent of the Second Amendment is to protect the individual's right to keep and bear arms, and that it is not connected to an individual's service in a state militia.

The Second Amendment protects the freedoms included in the First Amendment by providing the people the opportunity to, failing all other actions, throw off tyrannical rule by force, if necessary.

The anti-gun movement would establish stricter gun laws, limit firearms possession to police and other law enforcement agencies and eliminate the Second Amendment from the Bill of Rights. Some among the anti-gun movement believe that the Second Amendment is archaic, that individuals can not be trusted with firearms and do not need firearms for personal defense, home defense and defense against foreign or domestic enemies.

The Founding Fathers believed that an individual has "rights" and that a state has "powers." The right of the individual to keep and bear arms is a pre-existing right - based

---

[1]*District of Columbia v. Heller*, 554 U.S. 570 (2008). Web. 26 June, 2008.

upon a natural law from the Creator and not granted to individuals by a government. Les Adams traces the history of the right to keep and bear arms from ancient China through ancient Greece and Rome to England and America (17-161)[2]. The Second Amendment established the foundation for the people as individual citizens to keep and bear arms, and this positive law is not reserved for the states or for members of a state militia.

The gravest threats to the United States Constitution and to the First Amendment and Second Amendment are: federal and state governments that use their power to silence critical opinions thereby limiting freedom of speech and press that would adequately inform the public, large media corporations that silence investigative journalism and purposely shape public opinion, powerful political groups that restrict open discourse on contemporary issues, and groups of citizens that are openly hostile to other citizens who hold opinions different from theirs.

Summary

The most important documents in the cultural and political history of the United States are the Declaration of Independence, United States Constitution and Bill of Rights. The First Amendment and Second Amendment in the Bill of Rights, and the rest of the Amendments, are key to an appreciation of firearms ownership and use for personal or home defense and for defense of our free culture from domestic and foreign enemies.

To maintain a diversity of viewpoints in support of a free culture of American society, all citizens should continuously apply pressure on their elected representatives to uphold the United States Constitution and Bill of Rights.

---

[2]Adams, Les. (1996). *The Second Amendment Primer*. Birmingham, AL: Odysseus Editions, 1996. Print.

Quiz

1. What are the pillars of freedom from the First Amendment?

    a. Freedom of speech

    b. Freedom of press

    c. Freedom of religion

    d. Freedom of petition

    e. Freedom of assembly

    f. All of the above

2. The Second Amendment states: "A well regulated militia being necessary to the security of a free state, the right of the people to keep and bear arms shall not be infringed."

    a. True

    b. False

3. The Second Amendment protects the freedoms included in the First Amendment.

    a. True

    b. False

Chapter 2

Federal and State Laws

This chapter on federal and state laws pertaining to firearms only provides general guidelines. To obtain an accurate interpretation of the applicable laws regarding gun ownership and use, consult with a licensed local attorney with expertise in firearms laws.

Introduction

Laws at federal, state and local levels govern the purchase, sale, possession, ownership, use and transport of firearms. The United States Congress and the Supreme Court enact and interpret federal firearms laws, and these laws apply nationally. State legislatures and state supreme courts enact and interpret firearms laws that apply to their states. Some states have reciprocal agreements with other states to recognize as legal another state's valid handgun carry permit.

There are also ordinances and regulations concerning the possession and use of firearms on state and local properties. As an example, states may prevent or restrict possession and use of firearms within parks and forests. A private company may prevent its employees and customers from possession of firearms on its property.

Federal and state laws also govern the purchase, sale, possession, shipping and transportation of ammunition.

Firearms laws change over time and they vary from state to state. Legislatures and courts on federal and state levels pass new laws, and they revise and reinterpret existing laws.

Anyone who possesses a firearm has the responsibility to know what laws apply in order not to be found in violation of the laws by police and governing officials. Know the existing laws and keep up-to-date on the laws regarding possession and use of firearms.

One of the best sources for free up-to-date information about laws pertaining to firearms is the Internet website maintained by the National Rifle Association's Institute for Legislative Action at www.nraila.org. Join the NRA along with millions of other Americans to support its efforts to defend the 2nd Amendment and to enjoy a variety of benefits, including defense of the Constitutional right to keep and bear arms, magazine subscriptions, and insurance coverage.

Summary

Federal, state and local laws govern possession and use of firearms. Laws pertaining to firearms are different from state to state. Firearms laws apply to ammunition. Laws pertaining to firearms and ammunition change over time, including the interpretation of existing laws. The individual who owns or uses a firearm has the responsibility to know the applicable laws. Contact a licensed, qualified attorney to obtain correct information about specific firearms laws.

Quiz

1. Are state firearms laws the same from state to state?

    a. Yes

    b. No

2. Do gun laws, regulations and ordinances change over time?

    a. Yes

    b. No

3. What is the best source for free up-to-date information about firearms laws?

    a. Governor's office

    b. National Rifle Association

    c. Legislator's office

4. Who would be a good source to contact with specific questions about firearms laws?

    a. An attorney with expertise in state gun laws

    b. Another gun owner

    c. A gun salesperson

5. The gun owner is responsible for knowing the laws for possession and use of firearms.

    a. True

    b. False

Chapter 3

A Brief History of Guns

This chapter discusses basic facts about the origin and development of firearms. Topics include: invention of gunpowder, early gun firing mechanisms and modern firearm actions for revolvers and semi-automatic pistols.

Invention of Gunpowder

The Chinese invented "gunpowder" possibly as early as the 3rd century A.D. It is an explosive mixture of potassium nitrate, charcoal and sulfur. They used gunpowder for fireworks displays or religious ceremonies. They also used it for warfare as a signaling device, exploding grenades and to launch rockets into enemy ranks, causing injury and terror. The earliest firing devices were bamboo shafts and canisters that were charged with gunpowder, fused and loaded with clay balls, pebbles or small stones as projectiles. The loading process was done one part at a time. Ancient Chinese writings and paintings verify its discovery and use by the Chinese.

Transfer of Gunpowder to Europe

In Europe about the year 1250, Roger Bacon, an English Monk and early practitioner of the scientific method, produced a written record of gunpowder. Bacon likely learned about gunpowder from Arabs with whom he had been corresponding on scientific interests. Most likely, gunpowder came to the Arabs from the Chinese via the "Silk Road," an ancient trade route extending from Asia to the Middle East. in 1280, Bishop Albertus

Magnus produced the first European record of its use when recounting the siege of Seville, Spain that occurred in 1247. The English word "gunpowder" came into common use in the early 1300s. By 1350, the Europeans had produced an assortment of small and large canons fired by gunpowder for use in warfare. Ancient manuscripts report that by the 1400s German and French armies were using hand canons with barrels made of iron.

These illustrations come from a 1450 manuscript show soldiers using the hand cannon, which consisted of a metal tube with a touchhole at the rear for firing the charge. The hand canon was originally called a "gunne" (war machine) and was mounted on a short wooden pole. In time, this device became known as a handgun. As with earlier gunpowder firing devices in China, these ancient European handguns were loaded one part at a time, charged with gunpowder and a variety of projectiles that could travel a considerable distance, causing harm to an opposing army. Horse-mounted cavalrymen used the handgun during the Medieval period, when swards and pikes were still used for warfare.

Gunpowder, also known as black powder, was the only kind of explosive in use until 1884 when smokeless powder was invented in Europe.

Primitive Pistols

Historical records show that the town of Perugia, Italy ordered 500 hand cannons in 1364. Over time, the handguns were made smaller and smaller and in place of a metal tube strapped to a wooden pole, they had a handle or "stock" attached to the metal tube for easy gripping by the shooter. Gunsmiths invented a variety of firing mechanisms for the early hand cannons, including these:

- Burning stick or "punk" that fires the gunpowder charge at the touchhole (horse-mounted cavalryman).

- Burning wick attached to a pivoting bar that swivels into place to fire the charge at the touchhole (matchlock).

- Revolving, spring-loaded wheel that created sparks when rubbing flint against steel, igniting the priming powder at the touchhole (wheellock).

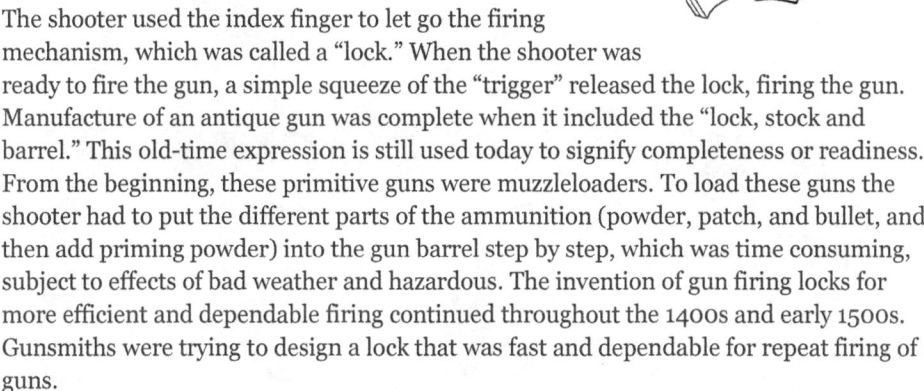

The shooter used the index finger to let go the firing mechanism, which was called a "lock." When the shooter was ready to fire the gun, a simple squeeze of the "trigger" released the lock, firing the gun. Manufacture of an antique gun was complete when it included the "lock, stock and barrel." This old-time expression is still used today to signify completeness or readiness. From the beginning, these primitive guns were muzzleloaders. To load these guns the shooter had to put the different parts of the ammunition (powder, patch, and bullet, and then add priming powder) into the gun barrel step by step, which was time consuming, subject to effects of bad weather and hazardous. The invention of gun firing locks for more efficient and dependable firing continued throughout the 1400s and early 1500s. Gunsmiths were trying to design a lock that was fast and dependable for repeat firing of guns.

Origin of the Word "Pistol"

The word "pistol" comes from the development of a small, lightweight and dependable wheellock hand cannon around 1540 in Pistoia, Italy. Over time the town's name was used when referring to a small gun that was made there, and the hand cannon has been called a pistol ever since.

Continuing Inventions to Fire Pistols

In pursuit of more efficient and dependable gun firing devices, inventors also developed the snaphance and miquelet locks. However, these were expensive and not very dependable. In the first decade of the 17th century, Marin le Bourceiys, a Frenchman, invented the flintlock, which soon became very popular in Europe and the Americas because it was more dependable and less expensive to purchase and maintain. The flintlock firing mechanism consisted of a falling, spring-loaded hammer that held a flint between its jaws. A squeeze of the trigger released the hammer, causing the flint to strike an iron frizzen and create sparks that would ignite the priming gunpowder in a small pan. The fast-burning priming powder flashed through a touchhole in the barrel's breech to ignite the charge in the barrel.

Colonials, Europeans and Native Americans on both sides of the wars in North America used the flintlock during the colonial period, the American Revolution and the War of 1812.

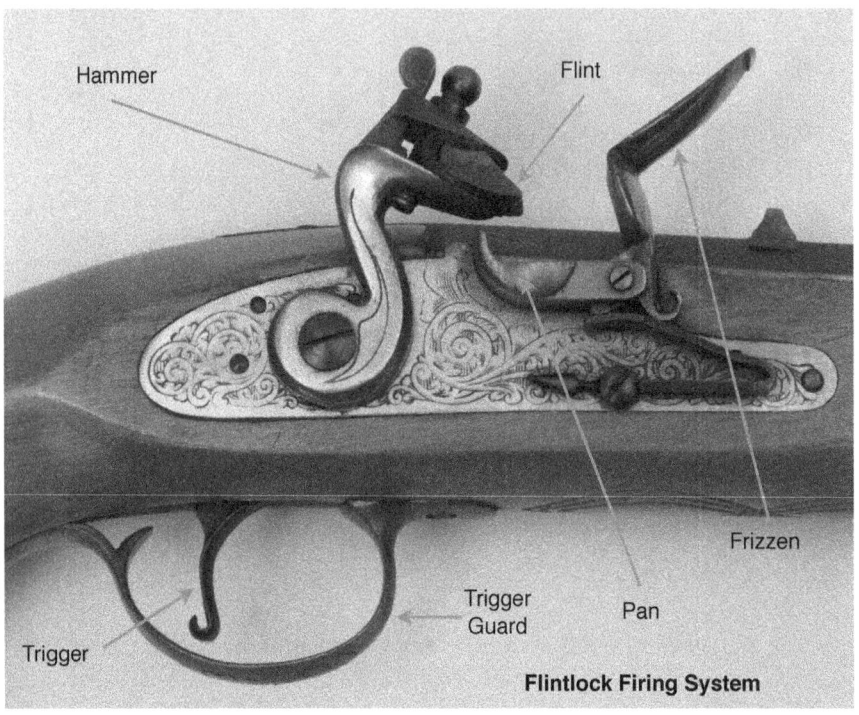

Flintlock Firing System

The invention and patent of the percussion cap in 1807 by Reverend Alexander Forsythe, a Presbyterian minister of Belhalvie in Aberdeenshire, Scotland is one of the most important advances in the history of firearms. Its simple design used a tiny brass cup with a small amount of impact-sensitive explosive material, fulminate of mercury. The percussion cap played a key role in the later development of the self-contained cartridge used for all modern ammunition.

With arrival of the percussion cap, the flint, priming powder, pan and frizzen of the flintlock firing mechanism were no longer state-of-the-art for firing guns. In their place was a small hollow, metal "nipple" screwed into the rear of the barrel. The percussion cap is placed on this nipple. When the spring-loaded hammer is released by a squeeze of the trigger, it falls on the percussion cap, igniting the explosive primer sending sparks through the nipple and into the barrel, firing the charge of gunpowder. Now, the percussion lock system was the preferred device to fire all guns: large and small cannons, rifles, shotguns and pistols.

Except for some guns equipped with multiple barrels, most guns were single-shot: after one shot the shooter must reload the gun or switch to a second loaded gun for repeat firing.

Early Repeating Pistols

On February 25, 1836, Samuel Colt of Hartford, Connecticut invented and patented one of the best and earliest repeat-firing pistols, which he called the S." Colt Revolving Gun." Colt established a company to manufacture percussion-type pistols, rifles and shotguns, all with the revolver firing system. The U.S. Army adopted his Colt-Walker Model pistol of 1847 for use by the U.S. Cavalry in the Mexican-American War. This handgun fired a .44 caliber bullet, held 6 shots in the chambers of a revolving cylinder, operated with a single action trigger and had a 9-inch barrel. The Colt-Walker handgun weighed 4 pounds and 9 ounces.

This type of pistol is a "percussion revolver."

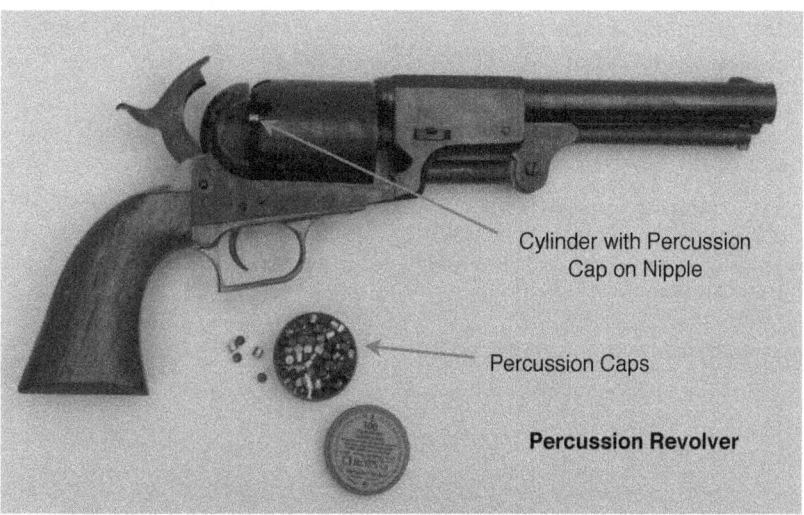

The distinguishing feature of all handguns of this type is the revolving cylinder, which is a storage device with several separate chambers that are loaded with gunpowder and bullets for repeat firing. Pulling the hammer back to the full-cock position rotates the cylinder so that the next loaded chamber comes in line for firing with a squeeze of the trigger.

Single Action and Double Action Revolvers

The operation of a revolver may be single action or double action. With the single action revolver, squeezing the trigger does one thing: releases the hammer to fire the cartridge. To get this type of revolver into the firing position, the hammer must be pulled back to the full-cock position first, then the trigger is squeezed to fire the gun. For the double action revolver, squeezing the trigger completes two actions: cocks and releases the hammer to fire the gun.

Self-Contained Cartridge and Smokeless Powder

In 1857 an important milestone in the development of firearms occurred: Smith and Wesson invented the first self-contained metallic cartridge as a .22 caliber short rimfire. The waterproof cartridge consisted of a case, primer, black powder and bullet. In addition to this cartridge, the company also began producing from 1857 to 1860 the S&W Model 1, called a "cartridge revolver," with 7 chambers to fire the rimfire cartridge. Seven cartridges, as self-contained, waterproof units, were loaded into the gun's cylinder, not as separate ammunition parts added one by one to each chamber. The pistol shooter was now able to rapidly load, fire and reload a gun by removing the fired cartridge cases and replacing them with loaded cartridges.

Using black powder to fire guns causes a number of problems. The burning powder creates a cloud of white smoke, which marks where the shooter is located. Also, the residue from the fired gunpowder is highly corrosive to metal. It builds up fouling material on the inside of the barrel and all moving parts with the firing of each bullet, reducing accuracy and hindering smooth operation of moving parts. Although Smith and Wesson's first self-contained metallic cartridge provided rapid loading, firing and reloading of the cartridge revolver, the fast buildup of residue from fired black powder required frequent cleaning of the handgun for accuracy and maintenance.

Modern Revolver

In 1884, Paul Vieille, a French chemist, invented smokeless powder. Its use to fire cartridges in guns made a profound difference in firearm designs and shooting - every kind of gun from cannons to pistols. When fired, smokeless powder develops heat and pressure sufficient for discharging a projectile accurately to a target over great distances. Unlike black powder, smokeless powder is clean burning and non-corrosive. Numerous shots can be fired accurately from a gun that has cartridges loaded with smokeless powder before it would have to be cleaned. In the decades since 1884, chemists have developed many different kinds of smokeless powder.

The most notable early revolver manufacturers in New England, in addition to Sam Colt's factory in Hartford, Connecticut, included Smith & Wesson of Springfield, Massachusetts, Iver Johnson's Arms and Cycle Works of Fitchburg, Massachusetts, and Harrington and Richardson Arms Company of Worcester, Massachusetts. Competing revolver manufacturers in Europe, mainly in France, included La Faucheux, Raphael and Perrin.

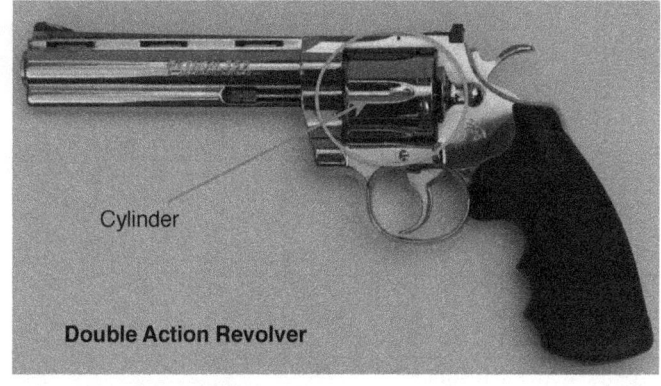
Double Action Revolver

Key developments in revolver design were the break-frame, hinged-frame, break-open, top-breaking or tip-up type revolver. All of these varieties provided dependable repeat firing for the revolver, but the number of chambers in the cylinder limit the revolver.

With a revolver, the cylinder is the storage device for all cartridges. Single-action firing of the revolver involves pulling the hammer to the rear to rotate the cylinder until a cartridge is in line with the barrel and to cock the action. Squeezing the trigger releases the hammer to fire the cartridge. The shooter continues this manual revolver firing sequence for repeat firing until all of the cartridges in the cylinder have been fired. With a double-action revolver, squeezing the trigger rotates the cylinder, cocks the action and releases the hammer to fire the cartridge. To continue firing either type of revolver, the shooter opens the action, removes all of the fired cases from the cylinder, reloads the cylinder with loaded cartridges, and closes the action in readiness for the next firing sequence.

Semi-Automatic Pistol

The first successful self-loading pistol was the C96 Mauser Military Pistol, invented in 1896 in Germany. Due to its unique grip, this gun became known as the "Mauser 1896 Broomhandle Pistol."

In 1902, in the U.S., John Moses Browning designed a semi-automatic pistol. With the pistol's firing mechanism cocked and a cartridge loaded in the chamber, the gun is fired with a squeeze of the trigger. Pressure from expanding gases of the fired cartridge operate the action automatically to re-cock the action, eject the fired case, load the next cartridge in the chamber and make the gun ready for the next shot.

With the semi-automatic pistol, a removable magazine is the storage device for additional cartridges. Cycling the slide backward and forward cocks the action and loads a cartridge from the magazine into the chamber, which is the rear portion of the barrel. One-by-one with each squeeze of the trigger the semi-automatic pistol fires a cartridge, automatically

Slide

Double Action Semi-Automatic Pistol

ejects the fired cartridge case and automatically loads the next cartridge into the chamber for another shot. After the last shot from an empty magazine the slide stays to the rear. For repeat firing, the shooter removes the empty magazine, inserts another magazine in its place full of loaded cartridges, releases the slide and continues firing.

Modern Single-Shot Pistol

The last example of a modern handgun is the single-shot pistol. This handgun is designed with either a break-open action or a bolt action. With a cartridge manually loaded into the chamber, the shooter takes one shot. For repeat firing, the shooter opens the action, loads another cartridge into the chamber, closes the action, takes aim at the target and squeezes the trigger. The single-shot pistol can be accurate to long distances and is especially popular for hunting and target or competitive shooting.

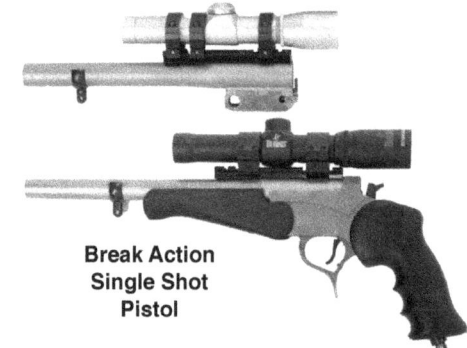

Break Action Single Shot Pistol

Today there is a wide variety of handguns that are manufactured by many different firearm manufacturing companies in the U.S. and other countries.

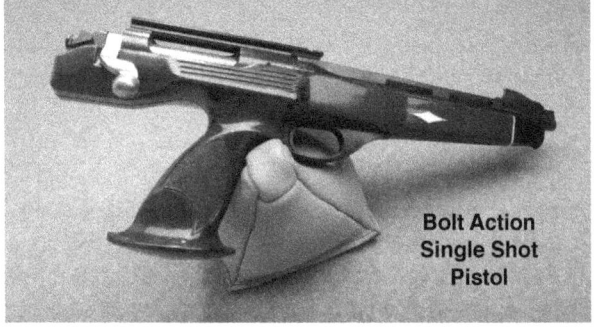

Bolt Action Single Shot Pistol

Also, the invention of different types of handguns and ammunition continues, leading to more and different kinds of each to support the diverse interests in shooting sports, personal defense, police work and military defense.

Summary

This chapter examined important historical facts in the development of pistols. Topics included invention of gunpowder by the Chinese, development and use of early hand cannons, single-shot black powder pistols in the Middle Ages, invention of various firing devices, actions for loading, firing and unloading cartridges, development of the self-contained cartridge and invention of the revolver and semi-automatic pistols.

Quiz

1. Historians report that the Chinese invented gunpowder more than 2,000 years ago.

    a. True

    b. False

2. Invention of the self-contained cartridge made possible rapid, dependable, repeat firing of guns.

    a. True

    b. False

3. Smokeless powder is preferred over black powder because it is clean burning and non-corrosive.

    a. True

    b. False

4. What is the distinguishing feature of revolvers?

    a. Hammer

    b. Cylinder

    c. Barrel

5. What is the distinguishing feature of semi-automatic pistols?

    a. Barrel

    b. Grip

    c. Slide

Chapter 4

Gun Safety Rules

This chapter is about firearm safety rules. There are four basic rules that everyone should know and follow whenever handling firearms. There are also nine additional safety rules that increase gun handling safety. There are safety rules for all live firing events and also shooting range safety rules. There are important firearm safety rules specifically for children.

Fundamental Firearm Safety Rules

- **A**ll guns are loaded.

- **C**ontrol the muzzle: keep the muzzle pointed in a safe direction.

- **T**rigger: keep your finger off the trigger and out of the trigger guard until ready to shoot.

- **T**arget: be sure of the target and what lies beyond.

To help remember these basic gun safety rules, memorize **ACTT** and use each letter to recall each rule.

The four basic safety rules apply to all guns, they are very important, they are related and every gun owner should follow them at all times.

Whenever picking up a gun, grab it by the grip, stock or barrel, do not touch the trigger or allow anything to touch the trigger, and keep the muzzle pointed in a safe direction. Then, open the action to inspect the gun for ammunition in the chamber, magazine and barrel. Remove all ammunition, unless the purpose for handling this gun is to shoot it.

The muzzle is the end of the gun barrel where the bullet exits when firing a cartridge. The muzzle of a gun is the ugliest hole in the world. Do not allow anyone to point a gun at you. Have control of the handgun for your personal defense and safety.

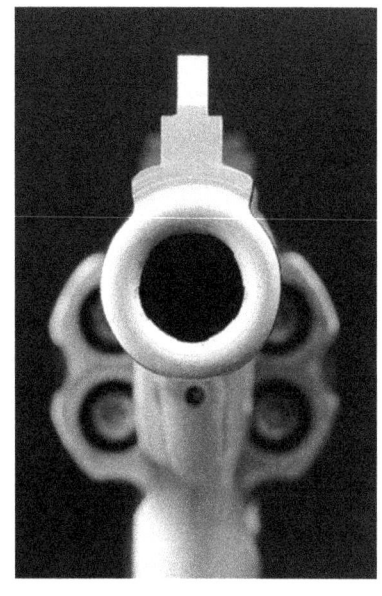

The bullet will travel to wherever the gun's muzzle is pointed when the gun fires and will stop when it has lost all of its energy. The speed of a bullet is very fast. A bullet fired from a gun has a tremendous amount of energy that can destroy many targets in its path until it comes to a stop.

Deciding what is a safe direction to point the gun's muzzle is difficult in most places. A shooting range is the safest place because it is set up for safe shooting exercises. At a shooting range the muzzle must be pointed down range where targets are set up for practice. Also, there is a backstop down range and backstops to the right and left sides to stop bullets and ricochets.

A safe place to point the muzzle of a gun for a safety inspection or for cleaning is difficult to determine in a house, apartment, store or place of business - anyplace where there may be other people, pet animals and farm animals. When using a gun for personal protection, it is extremely important that innocent people not be in the line of fire, including in different rooms and floors of a house because the bullet may travel through several walls and the floor or ceiling before it stops.

Whenever receiving a gun from someone else, insist that the other person keeps the muzzle pointed in a safe direction, does not touch the trigger with a finger or anything else. Require this person to open the action to inspect for ammunition in the chamber, magazine and barrel - before you touch it. Insist that all ammunition in the gun be removed from the gun before receiving it.

Additional Firearm Safety Rules

In addition to the Fundamental Firearm Safety Rules (ACTT), the owner of a firearm or the person in possession of a firearm should also follow these nine rules.

1. *Always keep the firearm unloaded until ready to shoot.* This rule applies in all instances to handling and storing a firearm unless the owner intends to use the gun for personal or home defense. Even so, the person who possesses the firearm has the responsibility to make certain that it is not accessible by unauthorized persons, including children, especially, but any person who should not be in possession of a firearm because they cannot be trusted with a firearm.

2. *Be sure the gun is safe to operate.* Always keep the manufacturer's instruction booklet for each firearm purchased. If the booklet is not available, use the Internet to locate the firearm manufacturer's website and search for the instruction booklet for that specific firearm. If the booklet is not available on the Internet, contact the manufacturer and request that a copy be sent to you by regular mail, fax or email.

3. *Know how to use the gun safely.* When purchasing a firearm, ask the salesperson to demonstrate how the firearm operates for loading, firing, reloading and unloading. Ask the sales person to show how to disassemble the firearm for inspection, cleaning and maintenance and how to reassemble the firearm. Ask the salesperson to explain the internal safety devices, and if there is an external safety device to prevent unintended firing of the gun. Ask how to operate this safety device. Ask what kind of ammunition is appropriate for that gun and what ammunition should never be used in that gun. Ask if there are any peculiar operational features of this gun and its use that the buyer should be aware of before using. Never use live ammunition to explore how to operate the gun. Use only training ammunition to discover how the gun operates and to determine if the gun operates properly.

4. *Use only the ammunition that is correct for the gun.* There are many types of firearms and many types of ammunition. A particular gun may be capable of firing a variety of cartridges. Ammunition can vary simply by the amount of powder or the bullet design. Different ammunition manufacturers make cartridges that vary by all of the different parts that make up a cartridge: case, powder, primer and bullet. Each cartridge is designed for a particular result when fired in a gun. Some cartridges of the same caliber as the gun should never be fired in that gun because they are too powerful. Use only the ammunition specified by the manufacturer for the gun. To determine what ammunition to use, consult the owner's manual from the manufacturer for that gun and match the information on the cartridge box with the barrel stamp on the gun.

5. *Wear appropriate safety devices for ear and eye protection.* The firing of a gun instantly creates a very loud noise. If the shooting is at an indoors range or under a

roof, the noise is greatly magnified. Wear hearing protection whenever firing a gun at outdoors and indoors ranges. Earplugs and earmuffs provide passive protection, cutting out all noises. Electronic hearing protection cuts out damaging noise but enables the shooter to hear voices. Also, the firing of a gun releases tiny particles of

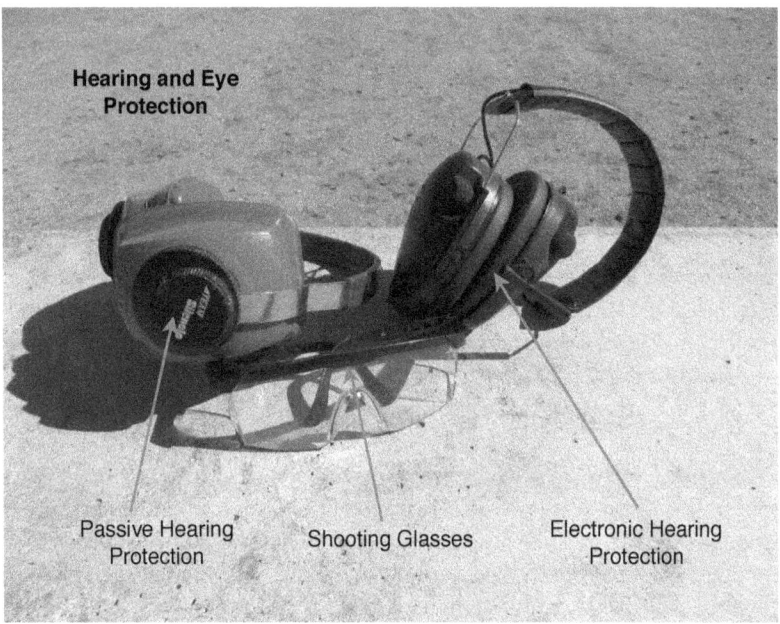

lead and other material from the burning powder. These particles fly out of the firearm action and may strike the face of the shooter or bystanders. Always wear eye protection whenever shooting a firearm and insist that anyone on the firing range, including spectators, wear hearing and eye protection at all times.

6. *Never use alcohol or drugs before or while shooting.* Consumption of alcohol or drugs, including prescription drugs, will impair an individual's normal mental processes (such as exercising judgment) and their physical movements (such as coordination of movement). Do not consume alcohol or drugs before or while shooting. Insist that other shooters at the shooting range not consume alcohol or use drugs before or during shooting.

7. *Store guns so that they are not accessible to unauthorized persons.* The individual who owns a firearm is responsible for the security of that firearm at all times. Persons who are not authorized to handle a firearm should not be able to gain access to a gun at any time. States have laws requiring safe storage of firearms by owners. Know the laws for the state where you live and follow those laws. Some firearms may be kept in a locked container, such as a safe or locking steel cabinet until they will be used for cleaning, inspection, practice, competition or hunting. Some guns may be intended for

personal or home defense and these guns may be loaded. Always make certain to secure all guns against access by unauthorized persons. Also, ammunition should be stored separate from firearms and secured from access by unauthorized persons.

8. *Certain types of guns require additional safety precautions.* Antique black powder firearms may have barrels that are not strong enough to withstand the higher pressures of smokeless powder. Some firearms have actions, frames and barrels that were designed to operate with standard ammunition only. Use of more powerful cartridges in these firearms may result in damage to the firearm and injury or death to the user or bystanders. Use only the ammunition that the manufacturer specifies for the firearm. Never use reloaded ammunition from another shooter. Read the owner's manual from the manufacturer to know how to use the firearm safely, including selection of the proper ammunition.

9. *Certain types of shooting activities require additional safety procedures.* At the shooting range, know the range safety rules and follow these rules at all times. Different shooting ranges may have different safety rules. For a formal shooting match there will be rules for the types of guns and ammunition permitted and for the operation and firing of the guns. Follow the range safety commands and rules strictly at all times.

Safety Rules for Live Fire Exercises

1. *Know the average velocity, maximum range and other characteristics of the ammunition for the handgun.* Use this knowledge to select the proper ammunition for purchase. Manufacturers make ammunition that may be used for different purposes, including target practice, competition, hunting and personal or home defense. A cartridge for target practice, for example, may have a "standard" load of powder and travel at a relatively slow velocity and short distance. A cartridge for hunting may have a +P or +P+ load of powder and travel at a very high velocity and a great distance. Also, bullets have different weights, shapes and parts depending on their use as determined by the manufacturer.

2. *Be patient and never be in a rush when shooting.* When shooting for recreational purposes, be calm and patient, never in a hurry. If there are personal problems or health issues, don't go to the shooting range. Get well first.

3. *If a cartridge fails to fire when the trigger is squeezed, stop shooting immediately and keep the muzzle pointed at the target.* When shooting, always pay attention to the feel and sound of the fired cartridge. If it did not sound or feel like it should have (a "click" instead of a "bang"), it most likely had too little powder, the powder is contaminated or the primer is defective - called a squib load. Stop shooting immediately. With the muzzle pointed down range and your finger off the trigger,

count off 30 seconds. The gun will fire within 30 seconds if it is a "hang-fire," meaning there was a delay in ignition of the powder. After 30 seconds this cartridge is a "misfire," meaning the cartridge is a "dud" that won't fire. In either case, after 30 seconds, open the action, remove any ammunition from the gun and - with the action open - push a cleaning rod down the barrel from the muzzle end to determine if there is a bullet stuck in the barrel. Inspect the cartridge to determine why it did not fire correctly and check the gun's action for good condition and proper operation. If there is any doubt about why the cartridge did not fire correctly, bring the gun to a gunsmith for inspection and repair.

If you become tired, stressed or inattentive, stop shooting immediately, pack up the equipment and return home. Take no chances with feelings of fatigue or anxiety when shooting firearms. Shooting is over for the day. When you are feeling well again, return to the shooting range for more practice.

Shooting Range Safety Rules

One of the safest places to enjoy the sport of handgun shooting is at an outdoor or indoor shooting range. These facilities may have individual shooting stations with target lanes, target stands and benches. Indoor shooting ranges may have automatic controls for posting and retrieving targets, sound baffles, air cleaning systems and air conditioning for heating and cooling. Also, at an indoor shooting range, the owner may provide gunsmith services, sell targets and hearing and eye protection, and sell firearms and ammunition.

"Firing Line" - The place at a shooting range where shooters line up left to right - in a straight line - to fire their guns at targets downrange. Except for indoor ranges where target retrieval systems are available, before anyone may step in front of the firing line to post or inspect targets, all shooting activity must stop and the entire shooting line must be inspected for safety: all firearms must be unloaded, actions open, empty chambers visible, magazines of semi-automatics out of the guns and safeties on (if so equipped). If there is anyone at any time that is in front of the firing line, no one at the firing line may touch firearms.

"Cease Fire" - During live fire activities where several individuals may be practicing their shooting skills, if the situation is unsafe for whatever reason, anyone present may call "cease fire" - loudly and clearly. At the "cease fire" command all shooters must stop firing immediately. Next steps are: keep your finger off the trigger, keep the muzzle pointed down range, open the action, remove all ammunition from chambers of revolvers and magazines from semi-automatics and put the safety "on" (if so equipped). All firearms should be placed on the bench, muzzles pointed downrange and with actions open and safeties "on." No one touches the firearms and no one resumes live fire activities until the safety issue has been resolved, and it is once again safe to resume shooting.

At indoors and outdoors ranges, there are additional shooting range safety rules for every individual to follow at all times. These shooting range safety rules may vary depending on the circumstances at the range.

If there is a formal shooting match, such as a National Rifle Association pistol match, a Range Safety Officer will be assigned to officiate the firing line until the match has ended.

Posted Range Safety Rules

Before any live firing begins in a formal shooting match, shooters place their guns, ammunition and other equipment on the shooter's bench. Guns are unloaded, with actions open and muzzles pointed downrange, chambers visible and safeties on (if so equipped). It is best to use an Empty Chamber Indicator (ECI) whenever not shooting the gun. Shooters then step back from the shooting line and wait for instructions. When the match begins, the range safety officer calls all shooters to the line. The commonly used commands for an official shooting match are:

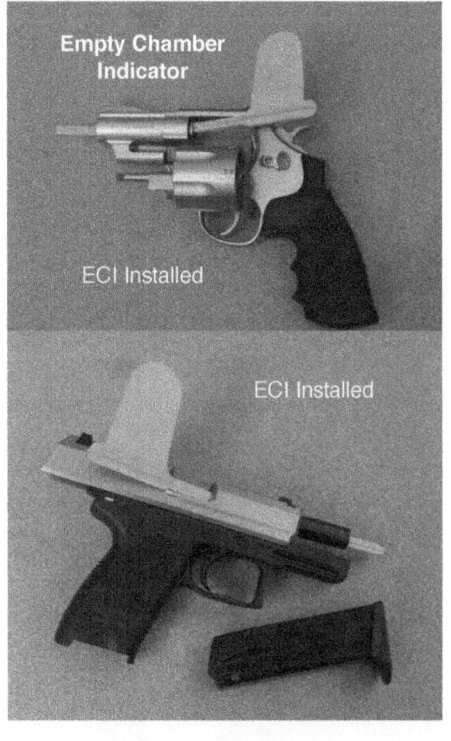

"Load" - With all shooters at the firing line, pistols on the bench, muzzles pointed down range, actions open, magazines out and finger off the trigger, the range safety officer gives the "load" command. At this time, the revolver shooters may place cartridges in the chambers, close the cylinder and raise the pistol to aim at the target. Semi-automatic pistol shooters may place a loaded magazine into the pistol, release the slide, take off the safety and raise the pistol to aim at the target.

"Commence Fire" - At this command, the shooters begin firing at the targets. The shooting range may have targets that are not visible to the shooters until they are turned for viewing at this command. Shooters may begin shooting as soon as the command is heard and the targets come into full view.

"Cease Fire" - At this command, all shooters must stop firing immediately, remove the finger from the trigger, keep the muzzle pointed down range, and wait for further instructions from the range safety officer. If there are no safety issues, the next command will be to open the action on revolvers and remove the magazine semi-automatic pistols, put the safety to the "on" position (if so equipped), make sure the firearm is unloaded, placed on the shooting bench with muzzle pointed downrange and step back from the shooting bench.

Indoors Range

The range safety officer continues with this sequence of commands:

"Is the range clear on the right?"

"Is the range clear on the left?"

"The range is clear."

"You may go forward to score your targets and post new targets for the next round." After all shooters have posted their new targets and returned to the firing line, the range safety officer issues these commands:

"Is the range safe on the right?"

"Is the range safe on the left?"

"The range is safe."

Indoors Range

"At the command, you may begin."

"Commence fire."

Any time that two or more shooters are practicing at a shooting range and there is no device for automatically posting targets, they should follow the above procedures. No shooter should assume that the other person on the firing line knows what should or in fact is going to happen next. All shooters must cooperate and follow the sequences above for posting targets and conducting live fire.

If there is any doubt about the safety of the shooting situation at any time, immediately call "cease fire" and make the situation safe before any shooting activities resume.

Firearm Rules for Children

Outdoors Range

Children know where everything is stored in their homes. Never doubt a child's ability to discover secrets hidden in the home, outbuildings or other places. When adults are away, the children may explore and get their hands on things that they should not be able to access, whether it is guns and ammunition, knives and other sharp tools, power tools and poisonous materials.

In order to prevent shooting incidents from happening where children are concerned, teach them when they are old enough to understand and to obey these firearm safety rules for children.

"If you see a gun:"

- *"STOP!"*
- *"Don't Touch."*
- *"Leave the Area."*
- *"Tell an Adult.*

These rules save children's lives. They are taught in the Eddie Eagle® Gun Safety Program of the National Rifle Association.

Summary

This chapter focused on rules for safe handling of guns. It is the most important chapter in *Handbook for Handguns*. Whether or not a person intends to own a firearm, following these rules when handling guns prevents shooting incidents.

The four basic firearm safety rules: **ACTT.**

- **A**ll guns are loaded.

- **C**ontrol the muzzle: keep the muzzle pointed in a safe direction.

- **T**rigger: keep your finger off the trigger and out of the trigger guard until ready to shoot.

- **T**arget: be sure of the target and what lies beyond.

At the "cease fire" command, all shooting activities must stop immediately. Anyone may call "cease fire."

Additional firearm safety rules expand upon the fundamental rules to provide greater assurances of safety.

Every shooting range has range safety rules, which may vary depending on the location and preferences of the range owners. Know the range safety rules and follow them at all times.

When shooting with others, always insist that everyone follow the range rules and commands, and also coordinate with the other shooters so that safety is assured throughout the shooting event.

The owner or the person in possession of a firearm is responsible for security of that firearm at all times. Firearms should be stored so that they are not accessible by unauthorized persons, especially children.

Teach children to follow the Eddie Eagle® Gun Safety Rules.

"If you see a gun:"

- **"STOP!"**

- **"Don't Touch."**

- "Leave the Area."
- "Tell an Adult."

Quiz

1. The A in ACTT stands for "All guns are loaded."

    a. True

    b. False

2. The C in ACTT stands for "Control the muzzle, keep the muzzle pointed in a safe direction."

    a. True

    b. False

3. The first T in ACTT stands for "Keep your finger off the trigger and inside the trigger guard until ready to shoot."

    a. True

    b. False

4. The second T in ACTT stands for "Be sure of your target, but what lies beyond the target is of no concern."

    a. True

    b. False

5. Who can call "Cease Fire" at a shooting range.

    a. Shooters

    b. Bystanders

    c. Anyone present

6. Eye protection is necessary for shooting sessions, but hearing protection is optional.

    a. True

    b. False

7. Shooters should not consume alcohol or illegal drugs before or during shooting, but prescription drugs, such as cold and flu medications, may be consumed.

    a. True

    b. False

8. Who would be an "unauthorized person" for access to firearms?

    a. Children under 18

    b. Elderly persons

    c. Visitors to the home

    d. Anyone without training

9. What rules should children follow if they discover a firearm?

    a. Stop what you are doing

    b. Don't touch the gun

    c. Leave the area

    d. Tell an Adult

    e. All of the above

10. The shooter should place an ECI (Empty Chamber Indicator in the gun when at the shooting range and not shooting.

    a. True

    b. False

Chapter 5

Revolvers and Semi-Automatics

This chapter provides an in-depth discussion of revolvers and semi-automatic pistols. The purpose is to identify and explain the most important parts of these guns, how they work and basic concerns for safe use.

Revolvers

The revolver is a pistol that has a cylinder with several separate chambers that hold cartridges for firing the gun. When a shooter pulls the hammer to the rear, the cylinder turns to bring a cartridge into alignment with the barrel for firing. Revolvers in common use may have as few as five to as many as ten chambers. A revolver that fires a cartridge having a small diameter, or caliber, such as the .22 caliber, may have ten chambers, whereas a revolver capable of firing the .357 Magnum may have five, six or seven chambers.

Parts of the Revolver

All pistols - revolvers and semi-automatics - have three main parts: frame, barrel and action. The actions of revolvers are distinctly different from the actions of semi-automatics. Also, the revolver does not have an external safety. Revolvers have internal safeties to prevent unintended discharge of a cartridge especially when the pistol is dropped.

Across the different types of revolvers there is a great degree of sameness, which makes the revolver easy to recognize and use. Recent innovations in revolver manufacture include modular designs so the owner can change parts. Other options may include installing a larger grip in place of a smaller one, light-weight materials for concealment and portability, and cosmetic differences where some parts of a revolver may have different colors - red, pink, blue, green, camouflage, etc.

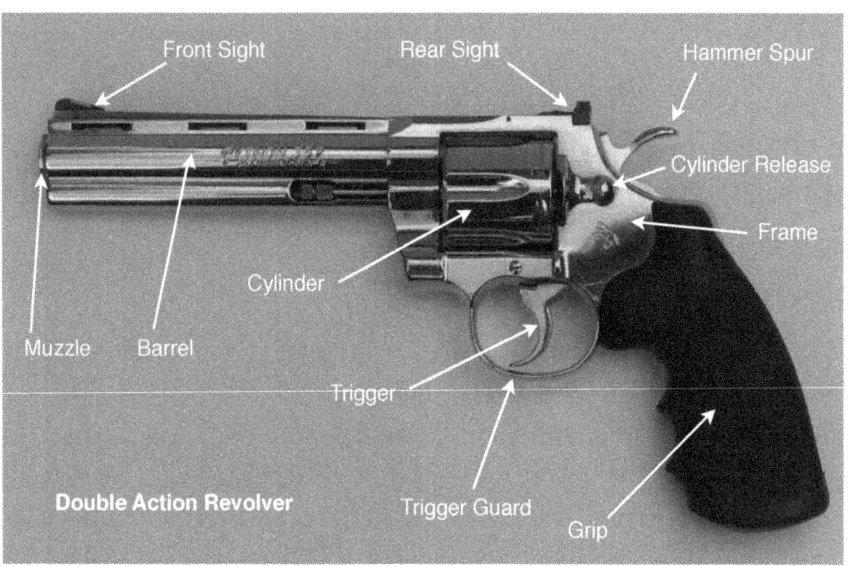

Double Action Revolver

Frame - The frame of the revolver is the unit that all of the other parts are attached to; like a person's spine everything else hangs off of it. Attached to or included inside the revolver's frame are the grip, trigger guard, sights, barrel and action.

☠ Grip: also called the stock, butt or handle attached to the rear of the frame for holding the revolver. The grip includes an external attachment made of rubber, wood, metal or other materials.

☠ Trigger Guard: a loop that is under the frame and inside of which is the trigger. The basic purpose of the trigger guard is to prevent unintended firing of the pistol from accidentally touching the trigger.

☠ Sights: devices that help the shooter align the gun barrel with the target for accurate shooting. With open sights, the rear sight is on the top of the frame above the cylinder and the front sight is on the top of the barrel near the muzzle. Open sights are either fixed or adjustable. There are also red dot sights, laser sights, telescopic sights and holographic sights.

Barrel - the metal tube attached to the front of a revolver's frame that the bullet travels through after the cartridge is fired. The portion just inside the rear of the revolver barrel is the breech or forcing cone that forces the bullet into the barrel. At the opposite or front end of the barrel is the muzzle where the bullet exits on its way to the target.

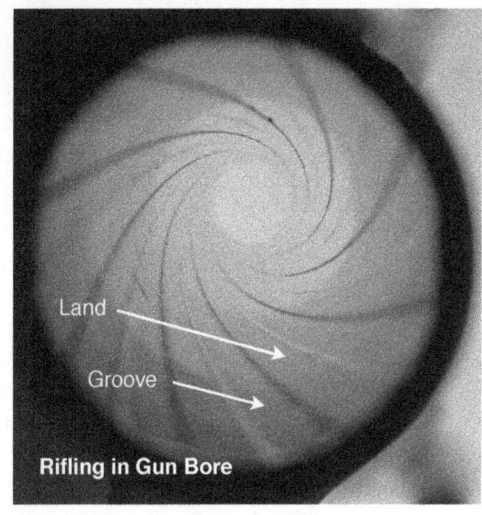

Rifling in Gun Bore

Inside of the barrel is rifling, which is a system of spiraling grooves cut into the inside surface of the gun barrel from end to end during the manufacturing process. Opposite each groove that was cut for the rifling is a land or raised ridge. The term for the whole inside of a gun barrel is the bore. When a cartridge is fired, the bullet passes through the bore, and as it moves the rifling grips and cuts into the bullet's exterior surface. This action puts a spin on the bullet that helps keep the bullet stable for an accurate flight to the target.

The inside diameter of the bore is the gun's caliber, which in the U.S. is a measurement from groove to groove of the rifling. Commonly in the U.S., the caliber of a gun is a measurement in hundredths of an inch. Examples of common calibers for pistols include .22, .38, .44 and .45, all decimals less than 1/2 an inch. When referring to these cartridges, the decimal is commonly omitted. A person may say: "twenty-two caliber" pistol or "forty-five" caliber pistol, for instance. The caliber of a gun may also be in millimeters, a common measurement of gun calibers in European countries and other nations. Examples include the 7 mm, 9 mm and 10mm cartridges.

Similarly, the outside diameter of a bullet is its caliber, measured either in hundredths of an inch or in millimeters.

Action - the set of moving parts that load, fire and unload the pistol. A gun's action includes assemblies of moving parts that are on the outside of the frame and other assemblies of moving parts that are inside the frame.

The external parts of a revolver's action include the hammer, trigger, cylinder release latch, cylinder, yoke, and cartridge ejection assembly. Inside the revolver's frame is an assembly of parts that operate together to rotate the cylinder and fire a cartridge when the hammer is pulled and trigger squeezed.

Additional parts of the revolver:

☙ Hammer Spur and Hammer: a curved metal piece that when pulled to the rear cocks the gun's action and, when released by squeezing the trigger, the hammer strikes the firing pin to fire a cartridge. The double action only revolver does not have an external hammer for cocking the action.

☙ Trigger: a curved metal lever that, when squeezed to the rear, releases the hammer to fire a cartridge.

☙ Firing Pin: a strong needle-like object that may be inside the frame or on the front end of the hammer. The purpose of the firing pin is to strike the cartridge primer with the impact of the released hammer to fire the cartridge.

☙ Cylinder Release Latch: a thumb-activated latch, also called a thumb piece, on the side or top of the revolver's frame that when pressed forward, inward or rearward releases the cylinder to swing it out for inspection, cleaning loading or removing cartridges.

☙ Cylinder: a round metal device with several separate chambers that are drilled through from end to end for storage of cartridges. The revolver's cylinder turns when the hammer is moved to the rear and this action aligns a cartridge with the gun's bore for firing.

☙ Yoke: an assembly of parts linking the cylinder to the frame. When releasing the cylinder latch with the thumb piece, the cylinder swings away from the frame on the yoke.

☙ Cartridge Extractor Assembly: a collection of parts that operate when the cylinder has been released from the frame. Pushing the extractor rod forces all of the cartridge cases out of their chambers for reloading the revolver.

Revolver Actions

There are three types of actions for a revolver: single action, double action and double action only.

Single Action

The old style single action revolver has two positions for the hammer: half cock and full cock. After pulling the hammer to the rear one click to the half cock position, the cylinder turns freely in one direction. Pushing open the loading gate on the right side of the frame at the rear of the cylinder when the hammer is in half cock allows inspection, loading, unloading and cleaning of all chambers while manually turning the cylinder. In order to operate the trigger, and to rotate the cylinder to bring a cartridge into alignment with the bore, the hammer must first be pulled to the rear to the full cock position - two clicks. In the full cock position the single action revolver is ready to fire a cartridge - with one slight squeeze of the trigger.

Squeezing the trigger on the single action revolver does only one thing: it releases the hammer to fire a cartridge.

Squeezing the trigger when the action is uncocked or in the half cock position will not cock or release the hammer to fire a cartridge on the single action revolver. The hammer must first be pulled to the rear to the full cock position, which cocks the action and sets up the trigger for firing a shot.

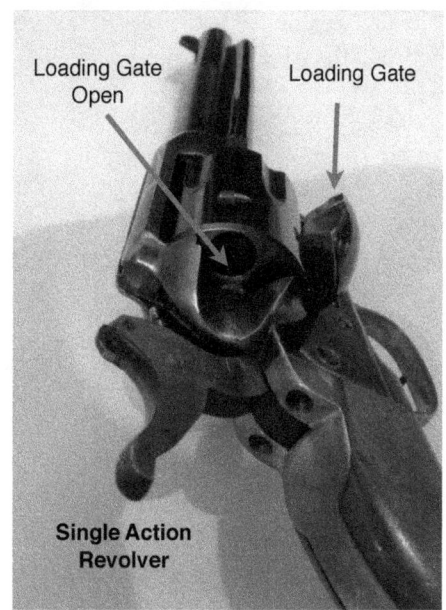

Single Action Revolver

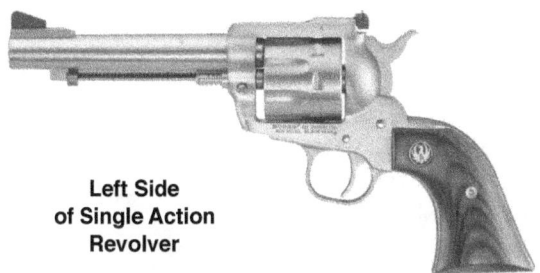

Left Side of Single Action Revolver

Double Action

The double action revolver does not have a half cock position. Pulling the hammer all the way to the rear locks the gun's action in the firing condition. Then, squeezing the trigger releases the hammer to fire a cartridge - single action shooting - same as with the old style single action revolver. Also, with the hammer at rest on the frame, squeezing the trigger on the double action revolver all the way to the rear in a single movement cocks the action and instantly releases the hammer to fire a cartridge - double action shooting. The double action revolver is capable of both single action and double action shooting. Squeezing the trigger for double action shooting is a much harder pull (12 pounds, for example) than for single action (2 pounds, for example). With single action shooting the hammer has already been pulled to the rear in the cocked position, ready to be released with a slight touch of the trigger.

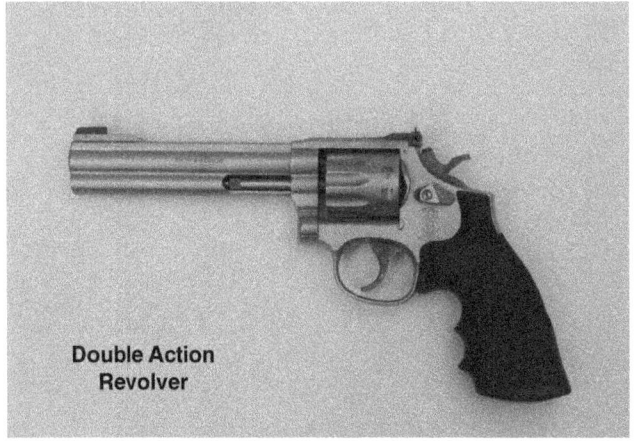

Double Action Revolver

The cylinder on a double action revolver swings out from the frame by operating the cylinder release latch. With the cylinder out, the revolver's action is open, which allows inspection of all chambers, cleaning, loading, and with a push on the ejection rod, removal of loaded cartridges or empty cartridge cases.

Double Action Only

The double action only revolver is similar to the double action revolver described above, with one important difference: this pistol cannot operate in single action. There is no external hammer to pull to the rear and cock the action. The only way the double action only revolver can fire is if the trigger is squeezed all the way to the rear in one movement to cock and release the hammer to fire a cartridge. Some double action only revolvers have no visible hammer; it is inside the frame. Others have a "bobbed" hammer, meaning a hammer is visible, but without the spur.

Double Action Only Revolver

The double action only revolver is a popular choice for self-defense because the hard trigger squeeze needed to fire the gun makes an unintended or accidental discharge less likely to occur. The double action only revolver does not have a hair-trigger release.

Loading and Unloading the Revolver

Action Open
Cylinder Out

To load the revolver, begin by following the ACTT rules. Never use live ammunition to practice loading and unloading a firearm. Use inert or training ammunition.

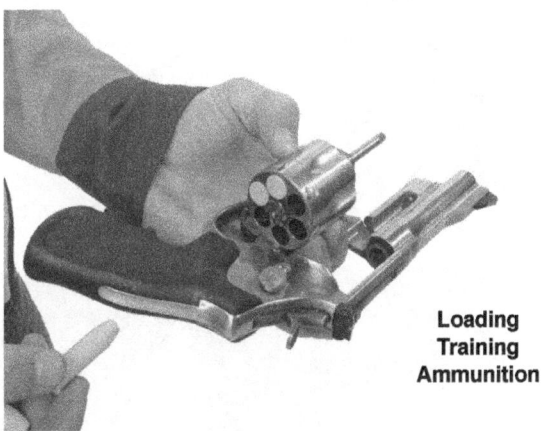

Loading Training Ammunition

With the muzzle pointed downward in a safe direction, operate the cylinder release latch with the thumb of one hand and push open the action with the middle fingers of the other hand. Inspect all chambers and the barrel to make sure they are clean and unobstructed. Select the correct ammunition based on the owner's manual from the manufacturer. With the muzzle pointing downward, load cartridges one-by-one into each chamber. Close the action by pushing the cylinder upward until it latches shut. The revolver is now loaded and ready for firing.

To unload the revolver, begin by following the ACTT rules.

With the muzzle pointed upward in a safe direction, open the action by operating the cylinder release latch. If the cartridges are clean and unfired, they will likely fall out of the chambers. If the cartridges have been fired, the cases will be stuck in the chambers because of swelling and fouling. Push the cartridge extractor rod to force all cartridge cases out of the chambers. Inspect chambers and action for overall condition and check the barrel for obstructions. Close the action. The revolver is now ready for storage.

Clean guns at the earliest opportunity after each shooting session to keep them free of fouling, grit and grime and in good working condition.

Decocking the Revolver

There may be times when you are shooting the single action or double action revolver and you have the hammer cocked but you do not want to fire the gun. In this case, you must use both hands to manually release the revolver's action from the cocked position.

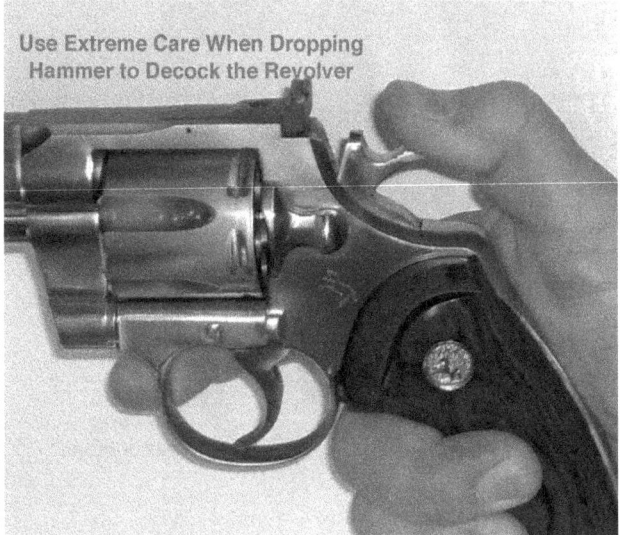

Follow these steps to decock the revolver.

1. Keep the muzzle pointed in a safe direction, your finger off the trigger and your finger out of the trigger guard.

2. With the shooting hand holding the gun's grip, place the thumb of the other hand between the hammer and the frame to prevent the hammer from moving forward. Use the thumb of the shooting hand to apply pressure on the hammer spur to prevent it from moving forward. Both thumbs are now in positions to prevent the hammer from moving forward. If the hammer slips from your grasp, in the next step, it will fire the gun.

3. With your trigger finger, gently squeeze on the trigger to release the hammer from the cocked position. Remove your finger from the trigger and take your finger out of the trigger guard.

4. With extreme care, keep your thumb on the hammer spur but ease the hammer toward the frame and at the same time gradually move your other thumb out of the way of the hammer to allow it to travel and come to rest on the frame. The gun is now decocked.

There is no need for a decocking procedure with the double-action only revolver because with every squeeze of the trigger the gun completes the firing sequence to cock and release the hammer to fire a cartridge.

Practice the revolver decocking procedure without ammunition in the revolver or use training ammunition until you have mastered this skill.

Also, during the decocking procedure the hammer may not complete its movement to where it comes to rest on the frame, but instead the action stalls part way. If this occurs, use your thumb to pull the hammer all the way back to the cocked position and repeat the decocking steps above.

Revolvers do not have external safeties. Follow these safety rules for storage and carry of revolvers.

- Never store a revolver in the cocked position.

- Never holster a revolver in the cocked position.

- Never carry a revolver in the cocked position.

Semi-Automatic Pistols

The distinguishing fact about the semi-automatic pistol is that it is self-loading. Each time the pistol fires, the gun's slide automatically moves to the rear, ejects the spent cartridge case, and pushes the next cartridge out of the magazine and into the breech of the gun barrel for the next shot. This firing, ejecting, loading, firing sequence continues with each squeeze of the trigger until the magazine is emptied of all cartridges.

Across the various models and manufacturers of semi-automatic pistols there is little sameness. All semi-automatic pistols have a feature that makes them distinctly different from revolvers: a slide that cycles to load, fire, eject and load cartridges. But the different handgun manufacturing companies produce different models and designs for their semi-automatic pistols, so even the design and operation of the slide may vary from model to model.

Parts of the Semi-Automatic Pistol

All pistols have three main parts: frame, barrel and action.

Frame - the structure that holds all of the other parts of the pistol together. The grip, grip panels, sights and trigger guard are attached to the frame.

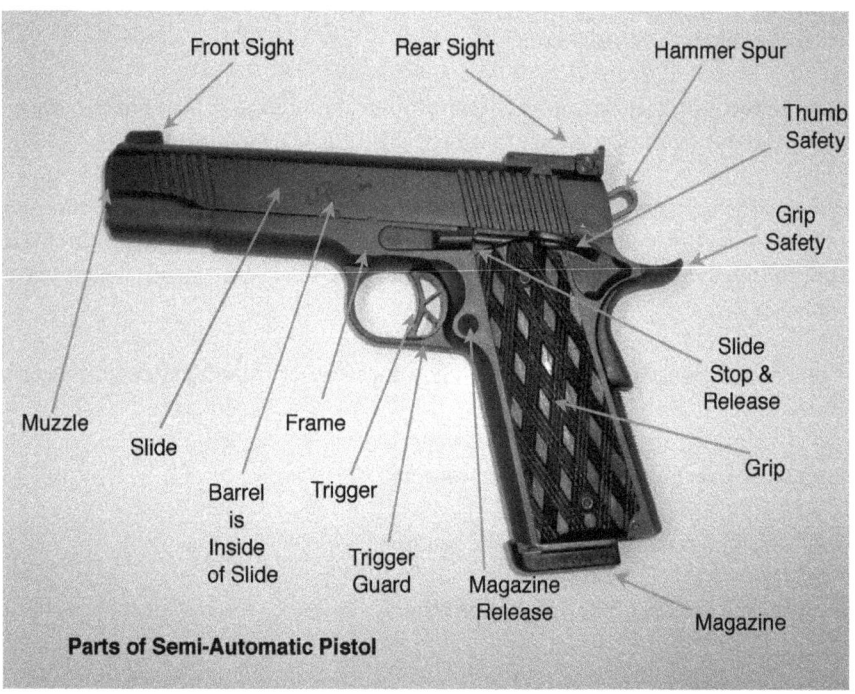

Parts of Semi-Automatic Pistol

☻ Grip: also called the stock, butt or handle attached to the rear of the frame for holding the semi-automatic pistol. The grip may contain separate panels on each side made of wood, metal or other materials.

☻ Trigger Guard: a loop that is under the frame and inside of which is the trigger. The basic purpose of the trigger guard is to prevent unintended firing of the pistol from accidental touching.

☻ Sights: devices that help the shooter align the gun barrel with the target for accurate shooting. For open sights, the rear sight is on the top of the slide and the front sight is on the top of the slide near the muzzle. Open sights are either fixed or adjustable. Other sights for pistols include red dot sights, laser sights, telescopic sights and holographic sights.

Model 1911 Semi-Automatic Pistol with External Features in Stainless Steel

Barrel - a metal pipe that the bullet travels through after the cartridge is fired. The barrel on a semi-automatic pistol may be loose fitting until the action is locked for firing. Also, the barrel has a single chamber (breech) for holding the cartridge until the gun is fired. From the breech to the muzzle the barrel is rifled. As with the revolver barrel, the lands and grooves of the rifling put a spin on the bullet as it travels through the barrel. Also, the caliber of a semi-automatic pistol is the measure of the inside diameter of the barrel from groove to groove, either in hundredths of an inch or in millimeters. And, as with the revolver, the caliber of the cartridge is a measure of the outside diameter of the bullet, in hundredths of an inch or in millimeters.

The semi-automatic pistol may be disassembled for cleaning and inspection. In the disassembled condition, the semi-automatic's parts may include the slide, frame, barrel, barrel link, recoil spring and recoil spring guide.

Action - a set of moving parts that load, fire and unload the pistol. Some parts for the action of the semi-automatic pistol are inside the slide and not accessible except by a gunsmith. Other parts are attached to the slide and frame and may be disassembled for inspection and cleaning.

Parts of the semi-automatic pistol include the following:

🔸 Trigger: a curved metal lever that when squeezed releases the hammer or firing mechanism to fire a cartridge.

🔸 Hammer Spur and Hammer: a curved metal piece that enables the shooter to cock the action for a shot. When the hammer is cocked and the trigger is squeezed, the hammer falls on the firing pin to fire a cartridge. Not all pistols have an external hammer.

🔸 Firing Pin: a strong needle-like part located inside the slide. When the trigger is squeezed, the firing mechanism strikes the firing pin, which strikes the primer of the cartridge to fire the powder inside the cartridge.

🔸 Magazine Release Button: a button or lever on the side of the frame near the trigger guard that when pressed releases the magazine from its position, commonly stored in the grip.

🌀 Slide: a hollowed out metal part that contains the barrel, firing mechanism, firing pin, recoil spring, and recoil spring guide.

🌀 Slide Stop & Release: a metal tab on the side of the frame that holds the slide fully to the rear in the action open position and when released allows the slide to move forward closing the action. When the last cartridge fires in a semi-automatic pistol, the slide stop locks the action open automatically.

🌀 Safety Decocking Lever: a lever that lowers the hammer from the cocked position to un-cock the action without danger of firing the cartridge. Not all pistols have a safety decocking lever.

🌀 Magazine: a spring-loaded storage device for holding extra cartridges in a semi-automatic pistol.

🌀 Thumb Safety: a mechanical device with a switch on the side of the frame that is designed to reduce the chance of unintended or accidental firing of the pistol. Not all pistols have external thumb safety devices.

Semi-Automatic Pistol Actions

There are three types of actions for the semi-automatic pistol: single action, double action and double action only.

Single Action

The trigger on a single action semi-automatic pistol does only one thing: releases the hammer or an internal firing mechanism so that the firing pin strikes the primer to fire a cartridge.

Smith & Wesson Model 41
22 Caliber
Single Action
Hammerless

After firing the first shot with this pistol, the gun automatically loads a second cartridge from the magazine into the chamber, and with each successive squeeze of the trigger the pistol fires until all cartridges have been fired or the shooter stops squeezing the trigger.

The hammer is cocked for the first shot by: (1) pulling back on the slide all the way to the rear with a loaded magazine in the gun and releasing the slide to put a cartridge into the chamber, or (2) if the firing mechanism was cocked by the slide action beforehand, but the hammer was let down, the hammer is pulled back by the shooter to cock the firing mechanism.

Squeezing the trigger when the action is not cocked will not fire the single action semi-automatic pistol.

Double Action

The trigger on the double action semi-automatic pistol completes two tasks: cocks the hammer or internal firing mechanism (double action) and releases the hammer or firing mechanism so that the firing pin strikes the primer to fire the cartridge. When the first cartridge fires, the gun automatically loads a second cartridge into the chamber and successive squeezes on the trigger (now single action) will fire the pistol until all cartridges have been fired or the shooter stops squeezing the trigger.

Kimber Model 1911
45 Caliber ACP
Single Action
with Hammer

Sig Model 220
45 Caliber Auto
Double Action
Hammer

Beretta Model 96
40 Caliber
Double Action
Hammer
Decocking Lever

HK USP Compact
40 Caliber
Double Action
Bobbed Hammer
Decocking Lever

Double Action Only

The trigger on the double action only (DOA) semi-automatic pistol operates only in the double action mode. There is no hammer spur to cock the pistol's action and shoot in single-action mode.

To fire this pistol, the shooter places a loaded magazine in the gun, pulls back on the slide and releases the slide to put a cartridge in the chamber. The action is not cocked, but there is a cartridge in the chamber. With a

Kahr Model PM40
40 Caliber
Double Action Only

double action (hard) squeeze of the trigger, the action is cocked and the firing mechanism released to fire a cartridge. With this first firing, the slide automatically puts a second cartridge in the chamber. With a second double action (hard) squeeze on the trigger, the second cartridge fires. This firing sequence with the double action only semi-automatic pistol may continue until all cartridges have been fired or the shooter stops squeezing the trigger. As with the double action only revolver, the double action only semi-automatic pistol is a popular choice for self-defense. With the hard trigger squeeze there is less likelihood of an unintended or accidental discharge. The double action only pistol does not have a hair-trigger release.

Loading and Unloading the Pistol

To load a semi-automatic pistol, begin by following the ACTT rules. Never use live ammunition to practice loading and unloading a firearm. Use inert or training ammunition.

Put the thumb safety in the "ON" position if so equipped.

Open the action by griping and pulling the slide all the way back until it stops with one hand and at the same time engaging the slide stop with the thumb of the other hand. Depress the magazine release button and remove the magazine. Inspect the slide, action, barrel and magazine for cleanliness and obstructions.

Model 1911 Semi-Automatic Pistol
Action Locked Open
Magazine Removed

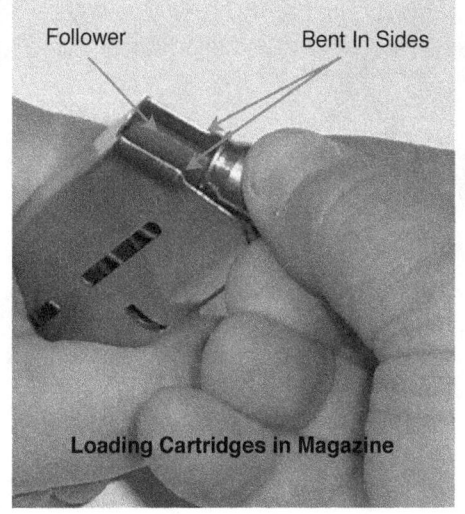

Loading Cartridges in Magazine (Follower, Bent In Sides)

Select the correct ammunition based on the owner's manual from the manufacturer. With the magazine removed from the gun and held firmly in the upward position with one hand, use the other hand to insert cartridges one-by-one into the magazine until it is full. This step requires depressing the follower and spring on the top, inside portion of the magazine so that the cartridges fit under the bent-in sides at the top of the magazine. Ensure that the cartridges face in the correct direction - the bullet must face where the muzzle would be when the magazine has been repositioned in the gun.

While holding the pistol grip with one hand, insert the magazine into the opening at the bottom of the grip with the other hand and push the magazine up firmly until it clicks into position. Grip the pistol firmly in one hand and while doing so use the other hand to grip the slide, pull the slide back slightly until hearing a click, and then release it. Do not touch the slide as it travels forward to insert a cartridge into the chamber. Doing so may prevent the action from fully locking into position and the gun will not fire. Follow this same rule when firing the semi-automatic pistol: never touch the slide. Another way to release the slide is to press the slide release tab so the slide moves forward to place a cartridge in the chamber. To unload the semi-automatic pistol, begin by following the ACTT rules. Put the safety in the "ON" position, if so equipped.

Loading Magazine in Gun

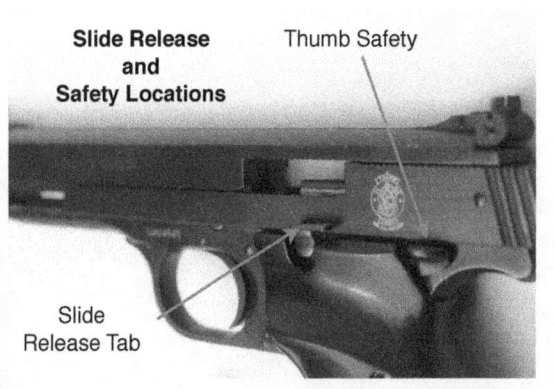

Slide Release and Safety Locations, Thumb Safety, Slide Release Tab

Open the action by pulling the slide all the way to the rear until it locks open. If the pistol has just fired its last cartridge, the slide is locked to the rear automatically. Depress the magazine release tab and remove the magazine from the pistol.

Inspect the magazine, action and barrel for overall condition and any obstructions.

After determining that there is no ammunition in the magazine or barrel, reinsert the magazine into the pistol, release the slide and check to see that the safety is in the "ON" position, if so equipped. Close the action. The gun is now ready for storage.

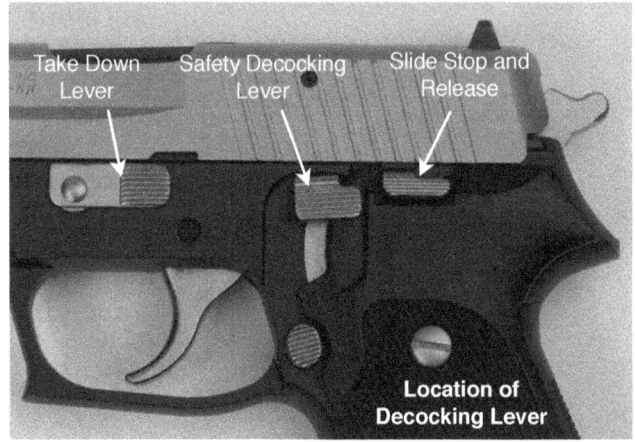

To keep guns free of fouling, dirt and grime and in good working condition, clean them as soon as possible after each shooting session..

Decocking the Semi-Automatic Pistol

There may be times when you are shooting a semi-automatic pistol when the gun has a cartridge in the chamber and the action is cocked, but you want to stop firing the gun.

Some semi-automatic pistols have safety decocking mechanisms to decock the pistol; others do not have a safety decocking mechanism.

To decock the semi-automatic pistol that is equipped with a safety decocking mechanism, follow these steps. Keep the muzzle pointed in a safe direction.

1. Keep your finger of the trigger and keep your finger out of the trigger guard.

2. If all shooting has ended, operate the magazine release button and remove the magazine from the gun.

3. While holding the gun's grip with the shooting hand, operate the safety decocking mechanism with either thumb to release the action from the cocked position.

4. The safety decocking mechanism may also have a position for engaging the safety. Put the gun's safety in the "ON" position.

If there is no decocking mechanism, follow these steps to unload the pistol.

1. Keep the muzzle pointed in a safe direction.
2. Keep your finger off the trigger and keep your finger out of the trigger guard.
3. Hold the gun by the grip with your shooting hand.
4. Operate the magazine release button and remove the magazine from the gun.
5. Operate the slide to eject the cartridge from the chamber and engage the slide stop latch to lock the slide back and the action open.

There is no need for a safety decocking procedure with the double-action only semi-automatic pistol because with every squeeze of the trigger the gun completes the firing sequence to cock and release the hammer or internal firing mechanism to fire a cartridge.

Practice the decocking procedure on the semi-automatic pistol without ammunition in the chamber and magazine or use training ammunition until you have mastered this skill.

Semi-automatic pistols present more options for storage and carry than revolvers because they have a variety of internal safeties, external thumb safeties and safety decocking mechanisms.

If the purpose of the pistol is to provide personal or home defense, these options, from higher to lower condition of readiness to fire the gun, are recommended:

- Cartridge in the chamber, full magazine in the gun, action cocked, thumb safety "ON," if so equipped.

- Cartridge in the chamber, full magazine in the gun, action decocked and thumb safety "ON," if so equipped.

- Cartridge in the chamber, full magazine in the gun, hammer is down and the thumb safety "ON," if so equipped.

- No cartridge in the chamber, full magazine in the gun, action is not cocked, thumb safety "ON," if so equipped.

- No cartridge in the chamber, empty magazine, action is not cocked, thumb safety is "ON," if so equipped.

The decisions about the pistol's condition for storage or carry should be made with care and practice.

Safeties on Firearms

The safety on a firearm is a mechanical device that is designed to help prevent the unintended or accidental discharge of the gun. A safety can fail to operate as designed. If the firearm has a thumb safety switch, keep it "ON," until ready to fire the gun, but recognize that it can fail. If the pistol has a decocking mechanism, decock the action when carrying or until ready to fire the gun. Not all semi-automatic pistols have an external thumb safety switch or decocking mechanism.

Summary

The three main parts of handguns are barrel, frame and action. Handguns with repeating actions are either revolvers or semi-automatics.

The defining feature of the revolver is the cylinder that has separate chambers to hold cartridges. The cylinder turns when the hammer is pulled to the rear and the action aligns a cartridge with the barrel. Revolvers are single action, double action or double action only. There is no external thumb safety on a revolver, but there are internal safeties to help prevent unintended or accidental discharges. The safety mechanisms in a firearm can fail to operate as intended.

The key fact about the semi-automatic pistol is its self-loading ability. When a cartridge is fired, the slide cycles rapidly backward and forward to eject the fired cartridge case and load the next cartridge from the magazine into the chamber for repeat firing. With each squeeze of the trigger a cartridge fires until all cartridges are fired or the shooter stops squeezing the trigger. Semi-automatic pistols are either single action, double action or double action only. Some semi-automatic pistols have safety decocking mechanisms or thumb safety switches. A safety on a firearm is a mechanical device that can fail to operate as designed.

Quiz

1. What are the three main parts of a handgun?

    a. Muzzle, trigger and grip

    b. Frame, barrel and action

    c. Barrel, safety and sights

2. The three different types of handgun actions are single action, double action and double action only

    a. True

    b. False

3. The trigger on the single action handgun does one thing: cocks the hammer to fire the gun.

    a. True

    b. False

4. The trigger on a double action revolver does two things: cocks the action and releases the hammer to fire the gun.

    a. True

    b. False

5. Which of the following is the double action only handgun?

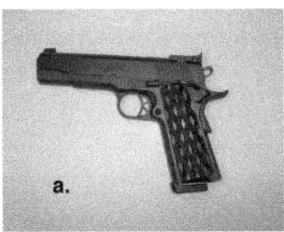
a.

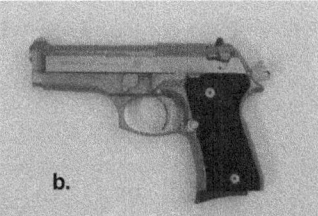
b.

c.

d.

6. The trigger on a double action only handgun completes the entire cycle for firing the gun, cocking the firing mechanism and releasing it to fire the gun.

   a. True

   b. False

7. Where are the cartridges stored in a revolver?

   a. Cylinder

   b. Grip

   c. Magazine

8. Where are the cartridges stored in a semi-automatic pistol?

   a. Slide

   b. Magazine

   c. Frame

9. The safety on a handgun is a mechanical device that can fail to operate as designed.

   a. True

   b. False

Chapter 6

Ammunition

This chapter describes the ammunition used in revolvers and semi-automatic pistols, including the parts of ammunition, varieties of calibers, powder loads and care of ammunition.

Parts of the Cartridge

There are four parts of ammunition for handguns.

- Case
- Primer
- Powder
- Bullet

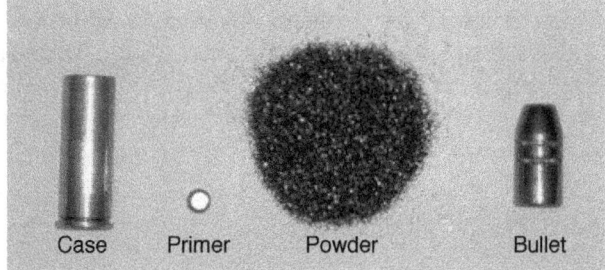

There are two types of cartridges:

- Rimfire

- Center-fire

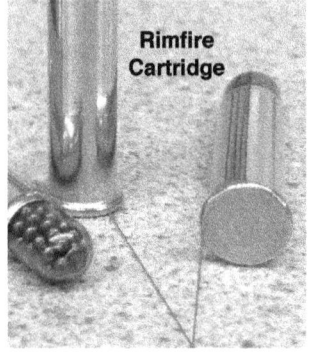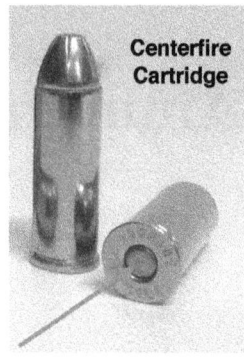

The location of the primer in the head of the cartridge case signifies whether a cartridge is rimfire or center-fire. As the arrows show in the examples above, the rimfire cartridge has the primer located inside the rim. The centerfire cartridge has the primer located in a tiny cap that is located in the primer pocket in the head of the cartridge.

Another term for a cartridge is round, as in :"I'm going to load another round."

Rim

Cartridges have various classifications based on their rims. This discussion will focus on rimmed and rimless cartridges because they are the most common types used in handguns.

A rimmed cartridge has a narrow extension, or rim, that extends outward from the head of the case and supports extraction of the case from the chamber of the gun, as found on the 22 caliber cartridge. The rimmed cartridge is commonly used in revolvers. The action of a revolver includes an ejector rod. With the action open and cylinder out, pushing the ejector rod extends the star-shaped extractor that catches the rim to force all of the cartridge cases out of their chambers at once.

A rimless case has an extracting groove just in front of the cartridge head that supports ejection of the case from the chamber of the gun, as found on the 45 Auto cartridge. Rimless cartridges are commonly used in semi-automatic pistols. When the pistol is fired, the slide moves to the rear and the extractor catches the groove on the cartridge case to pull it out of the chamber.

Rimfire Cartridge

The rimfire cartridge has the detonating primer compound on the inside of the rim. A cartridge fires when the firing pin strikes the rim of the case to detonate the primer and ignite the powder. The only rimfire cartridges manufactured today are the varieties of .22

caliber cartridges in different lengths and ranging from standard to magnum loads, and also the .17 caliber magnum rimfire cartridge.

Varieties of Rimfire Cartridges

There are four different .22 caliber rimfire cartridges commonly used in handguns, varying by case length and power from the short to the magnum.

- .22 Caliber Short
- .22 Caliber Long
- .22 Caliber Long Rifle
- .22 Caliber Winchester Magnum Rimfire (WMR)

22 Caliber WMR

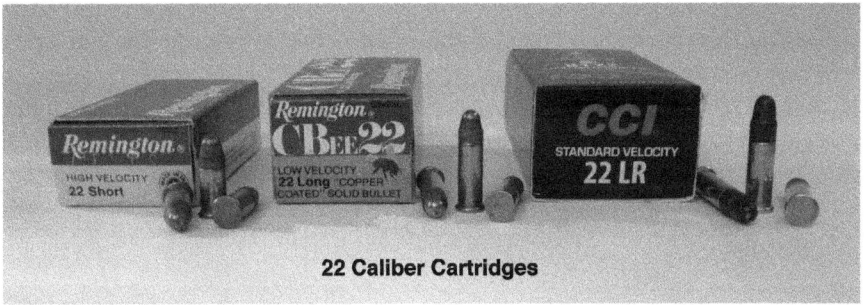

22 Caliber Cartridges

Manufacturers make .22 caliber rimfire cartridges in standard, high velocity and magnum loads. Bullet weights also vary from 29 to 50 grains. Although the cartridge is small, it is a popular choice for a wide range of uses, including personal defense, hunting, target shooting, plinking, and competitive shooting. The .22 caliber subsonic ammunition is popular for dispatching varmints in the backyard, because its report is relatively quiet. Also, the .22 caliber long rifle cartridge is available with a hollow plastic bullet that is filled with lead shot. This cartridge has a short effective range and is useful for dispatching mice and other varmints in outbuildings and grain bins so as not to damage walls.

Center Fire Cartridge

The center-fire cartridge has the primer located in the center of the cartridge head. This primer is a separate device that looks like a tiny metal cup. Inside this primer is a small pellet of priming compound and an anvil. To fire the center-fire cartridge, the gun's firing pin strikes the primer cup, the anvil crushes the priming compound causing it to explode, which ignites the powder.

Varieties of Center Fire Cartridges

There are more centerfire cartridges for handguns than are included in this discussion, and the invention of new cartridges continues, guaranteeing there will be an even greater variety in the future. Some cartridges are used exclusively in revolvers or single shot pistols, others exclusively in semi-automatics and some may be used in all types of handguns. The barrels, cylinders and magazines of some handguns can accept or be exchanged for others to accommodate a variety of cartridges. For example, the Governor by S&W, a revolver, accepts .410 shotshells, .45 ACP cartridges and .45 Long Colt cartridges.

The selection of any handgun is linked to the choice of the cartridge for the gun, and both of these decisions are dependent on one or more purposes that the owner may have for the handgun. Common uses for handguns are: personal defense, home defense, hunting, target shooting and competitive shooting. Smaller cartridges are used in guns with smaller, lighter frames, actions and barrels; larger cartridges require guns with larger and stronger frames, actions and barrels. The cartridge powder loads, including standard, +P and +P+ levels influence the gun's design and the gun owner's choices.

Many of the cartridges in this discussion can serve well for personal or home protection. The largest cartridges are especially popular for hunting big game, for police and military operations and for home defense. The handguns that fire them might be too heavy and bulky to carry for personal defense, except when traveling in wilderness areas. Recent advances in metallurgy have produced strong, lightweight materials, which can reduce the overall weight of firearms of all sizes.

Head Stamp

The closed end of a cartridge case is the head. The manufacturer may stamp identifying information on the head. As an example, .357 MAG REM signifies that the cartridge is a .357 magnum cartridge that was made by the Remington Arms Company. Cartridge head stamp information helps prevent the use of incorrect ammunition in a handgun.

Ammunition Loads

The load of a cartridge concerns the measured amount of powder placed in each cartridge case during manufacture. Factory-produced handgun ammunition is available in a variety of loads:

- Standard: an amount of powder loaded into a cartridge to create standard or baseline internal pressure. Standard ammunition may be fired in all revolvers and many semi-automatics. Some semi-automatic pistols require more powerful loads to cycle the action properly.

- +P (Plus-P): a cartridge that has an additional measure of powder added to the load to produce more internal pressure and heat when fired, which can support use of a heavier bullet and create higher bullet velocity.

- +P+ (Plus-P-Plus): a cartridge that has an even greater additional measure of powder (more than +P) added to the load to produce more internal pressure and heat when fired, which creates higher bullet velocity.

Firing a +P or a +P+ cartridge in a handgun that was designed for standard ammunition may damage the firearm and cause serious injury or death to the shooter and bystanders. Consult the owner's manual from the manufacturer to determine what type of ammunition is correct for the firearm before loading and shooting.

The original factory box for cartridges will specify the type of load that was used for all cartridges in that box. Always store ammunition in the original factory box to avoid confusion.

Common Handgun Cartridges

This discussion begins with the smallest caliber centerfire cartridge (25 ACP), about a quarter of an inch in diameter, and ends with the largest caliber (500 S&W), half an inch in diameter. The names of cartridges may indicate the manufacturer, inventor or their use in a type of firearm, for example, ACP - Automatic Colt Pistol, Casull - the inventor's name, Remington - manufacturer, Ruger - manufacturer, Sig - manufacturer, and Smith & Wesson - manufacturer.

25 ACP: smallest of common centerfire cartridges for semi-automatic pistols.

380 ACP: also called the 9mm Browning Short. The 380 is commonly used in semi-automatic pistols.

9mm Luger (Parabellum): also called 9mm or the 9. Adopted by German Army in 1908. Commonly used in Europe. Adopted by U.S. military in 1985 for M9 Beretta pistol.

38 Special: commonly used pistol cartridge for civilian military and police. Developed by Smith & Wesson in 1902. The 38 Special can be loaded in a 357 Magnum revolver.

357 Magnum: was developed by Smith & Wesson in 1935. It develops greater velocity than the 38 Special cartridge.

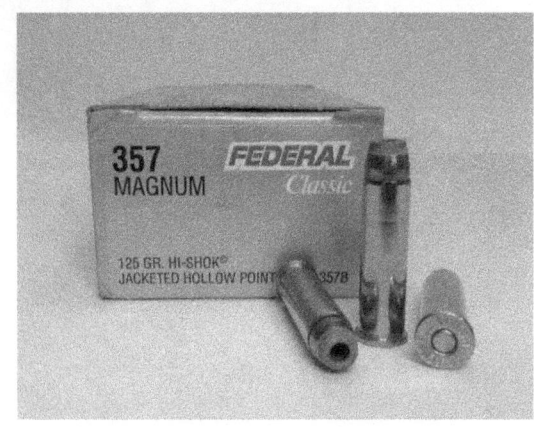

40 Smith & Wesson: was introduced by Smith & Wesson and Winchester for semi-automatic pistols in 1990. A popular choice by civilians, police and military because of greater stopping power than the 9mm. Has greater magazine capacity than 45 ACP and overall smaller size.

44 S&W Special: was developed to provide citizens, police and the military with a more powerful cartridge than the 38 Special. Has less recoil than the 44 Remington Magnum. It can be loaded into a 44 Magnum Revolver.

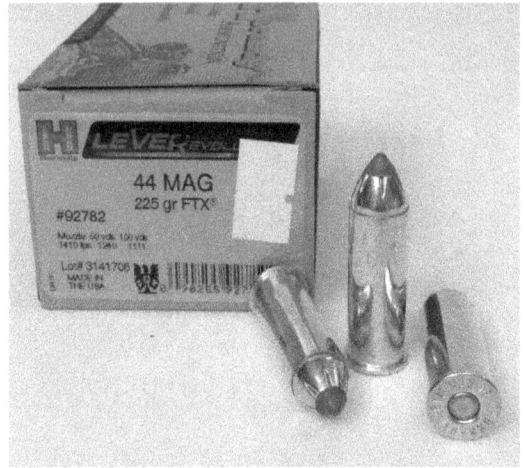

44 Remington Magnum: was introduced in 1954. Smith & Wesson and Remington developed this cartridge to be the best big game hunting cartridge. 44 Remington Magnum is a popular choice among hunters who use it for hunting big game.

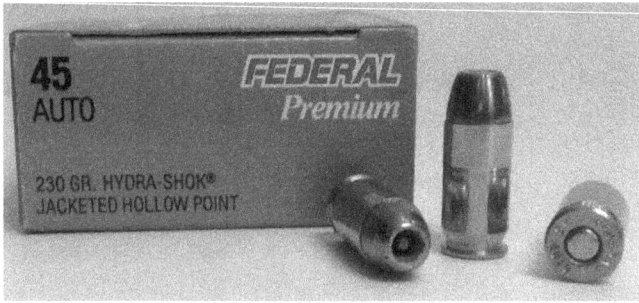

45 ACP: was first introduced in 1905 by John Moses Browning and matched up in 1911 with the M1911 45 semi-automatic pistol. U.S. military forces from WWI to the present time have used this cartridge. It is a popular cartridge among civilians, police and the military.

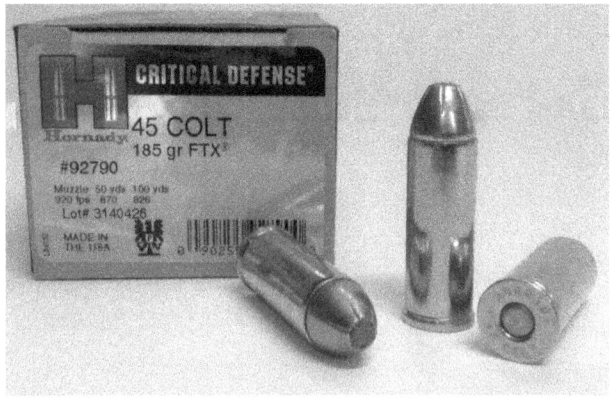

45 Colt (45 Long Colt or 45LC): first introduced in 1872 as a black powder cartridge.was originally developed for the Colt Single Action Army Revolver. The 45 Colt is a magnum level handgun cartridge that continues to be popular for target shooting and hunting.

454 Casull: was developed in 1957 by Dick Casull and Jack Fullmer. It was the first big bore caliber to break the record held by the 44 Remington Magnum. The 454 Casull is a massive, powerful choice for big game hunting.

460 S&W: is a longer and more powerful (called super magnum) version of the 454 Casull, which is longer and more powerful than the 45 Colt. This cartridge is popular for target shooting and hunting.

480 Ruger: is a magnum load version of the 454 Casull. This cartridge is popular for target shooting and hunting.

500 S&W: Smith & Wesson developed the 500 S&W in 2003. 500 S&W is a "hunting handgun for any animal walking," according to the company. 500 S&W took over status from the 44 Remington Magnum as the most powerful production handgun in the world. It is popular for target shooting and hunting, although its recoil is very substantial.

410 shotgun cartridge: has the same external dimensions as the 45 ACP and 45 Colt. This example is designed mainly for personal defense and may be loaded into the Smith & Wesson Governor Model and the Taurus Judge Public Defender revolvers.

Care of Ammunition

Handle ammunition only when inspecting it and when loading it into a firearm. Natural oils and salts from your skin can cause the metallic cases to corrode, making the cartridge difficult to operate in a firearm, especially a semi-automatic pistol.

Observe these rules when handling ammunition:

- Store ammunition in the original factory box or carton.

- Store ammunition in a cool, dry place, free from moisture and solvents or other chemicals.

- Wipe fingerprints from ammunition with a dry cloth.

- Store ammunition so that it is not accessible by unauthorized persons, especially children.

Results of contaminated cartridges include:

- Corrosion that prevents the cartridge from fitting into the chamber.

- Misfire - failure of a cartridge to fire when struck by the firing pin - after a 30 second wait.

- Hangfire - delay in the ignition of a cartridge when struck by the firing pin, but the cartridge fires within 30 seconds.

- Squib Load - development of less-than-normal pressure within the cartridge when struck by the firing pin.

When shooting firearms, listen carefully for the quality of the sound and at the same time pay attention to the feel of the gun when it fires. If it does not sound right (sound is too quiet or too loud) or feel right (recoil is too light, too heavy or delayed ignition), it was very likely a contaminated cartridge - but it fired (hangfire or squib load). Stop shooting immediately, keep the muzzle pointed in a safe direction, wait 30 seconds, open the action, remove all ammunition and determine the cause of the problem.

When a cartridge does not fire (misfire), stop shooting, keep the muzzle pointed in a safe direction, wait 30 seconds, and if there is no firing of the cartridge, open the action and remove all ammunition. Inspect the failed cartridge to determine what may have caused it to misfire.

Always take a cleaning rod to the shooting range when practicing. When a cartridge does not fire as expected, wait 30 seconds, unload the firearm, open the action and push the cleaning rod through the barrel to determine if the bullet is stuck in the barrel. If so, a gunsmith's services may be required to remove the stuck bullet from the barrel.

A significantly louder than normal shot and heavier than normal recoil can damage the firearm and cause harm to the shooter or bystanders. If this occurs, stop shooting immediately, give emergency assistance to anyone who may have been injured and determine if the firearm has been damaged. A gunsmith's services may be necessary to assure safe use.

Summary

Cartridge is the specific term for individual pieces of ammunition. Round and bullet are used as slang terms for a cartridge. Cartridges for handguns come in a wide variety of calibers and loads, but are classified into two categories: rimfire cartridges and center-fire cartridges. The calibers of cartridges vary from the small .17 Magnum Rimfire to the large 500 Smith & Wesson.

Gun manufacturers produce a wide variety of revolvers and semi-automatic pistols, each one designed to fire one kind of cartridge, although some handguns are designed to fire two or more different cartridges. Always check the barrel stamp and consult the owner's manual from the manufacturer for the correct ammunition to use in the handgun. Always store the ammunition in its original box or carton, keep it in a clean, cool, dry place and prevent access to the ammunition by unauthorized persons, especially children.

Quiz

1. Of the four parts that are used to make a self-contained cartridge, which contains all others?

    a. Case

    b. Primer

    c. Bullet

2. Where is the priming compound located in the rimfire cartridge?

    a. Head

    b. Brass

    c. Rim

3. Where is the primer located in a centerfire cartridge?

    a. Case mouth

    b. Primer pocket

    c. Rim

4. Ammunition should be stored in its original factory box or carton to prevent mixing different cartridges.

    a. True

    b. False

5. Store ammunition in a cool, dry place, free from moisture and solvents or other chemicals.

    a. True

    b. False

6. A cartridge is declared a misfire when it fails to fire after pulling the trigger and the shooter waits 30 seconds to ensure it is not a hangfire.

    a. True

    b. False

7. A cartridge that fails to fire immediately after squeezing the trigger, but fires within seconds is a hangfire.

    a. True

    b. False

8. What is a squib load?

    a. A cartridge loaded with too much powder making an extra loud noise

    b. A cartridge that fails to fire after waiting 30 seconds

    c. A cartridge that fires but may have had too little powder or contaminated powder

9. In the event that a cartridge does not sound or feel right, wait 30 seconds and then open the action, unload all cartridges and inspect the action and the bore.

    a. True

    b. False

Chapter 7

Ballistics

This discussion of ballistics concerns the movement of a bullet after a cartridge is fired in a gun - its travel through the barrel, the air and the target. Gravity pulls all objects in the earth's atmosphere to earth. Gravity pulls an apple downward as it falls from a tree, a basketball into the hoop, a golf ball to the green after teeing off, and in the same way pulls a bullet to the ground.

Interior Ballistics

Interior ballistics concerns what takes place inside the firearm when the firing pin strikes the primer of the cartridge.

At the instant that the firing pin strikes the primer, a very rapid sequence of events occurs.

- Primer creates a tiny explosion, creating intense heat.

- Powder begins to burn, creating heat and expanding gas.

- Pressure and heat from the burning powder force the bullet out of the cartridge case and into the barrel.

- Bullet travels through the barrel in a spinning motion, due to the rifling.

- Bullet exits the barrel at the muzzle.

Exterior Ballistics

When the bullet leaves the muzzle, it is spinning because of the rifling, and continues in this manner of flight until reaching the target. Gravity continuously pulls the bullet down, and air resistance and objects in the path of the bullet may disrupt its flight.

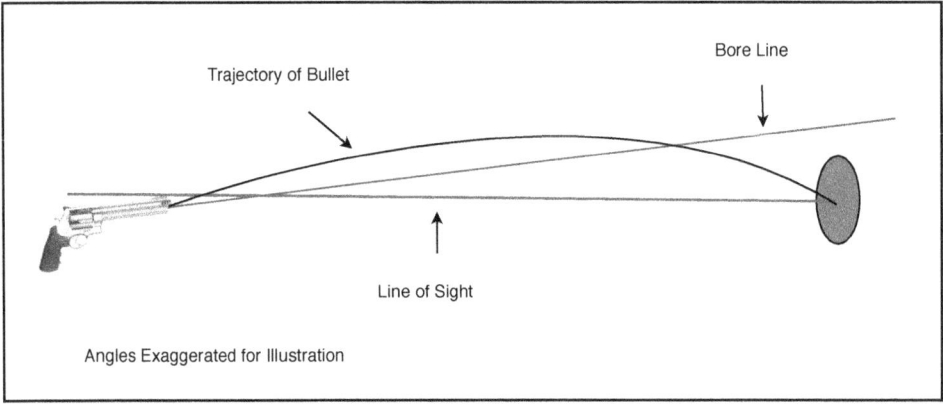

The downward force of gravity on the bullet causes its path or trajectory to be a curve, not a straight line. The shooter's line of sight is not affected by gravity and sees the target straight ahead. When firing a cartridge with the barrel in a position parallel to the line of sight, the bullet would exit the muzzle and gravity would immediately pull the bullet downward to hit low on the target or strike the ground under the target.

In order to obtain greater bullet travel distance and accuracy with the target, the gun barrel (bore line) must be set on an upward angle.

That is one of the purposes of sights on a gun - adjustments for elevation to compensate for constant gravitational pull on the bullet. By angling the barrel upward, the bullet travels out to a greater distance to hit the intended target, depending on the type and amount of gunpowder, air resistance and any objects in its path to the target. The other important purpose of sights on a gun is to adjust for windage - correcting the flight of the bullet to the target, more to the right or left, based on straightness of the barrel, its fit in the gun and the effects of wind.

Terminal Ballistics

When the bullet strikes the target its flight is finished, but its work is not done. Terminal ballistics defines what happens to the bullet when it first strikes the target - transferring its energy to the target - until it comes to rest in the target or it continues to something beyond the target.

Manufacturers design bullets with different kinds of materials and features that produce different results when they strike targets. Terminal ballistics is important to hunters, for example, because the velocity of the bullet and its behavior when it hits a game animal will determine if this was a humane, quick kill, which is desired. When the bullet strikes the game animal, the impact of the shot, expansion of the bullet and the depth and width of the wound channel can break bones and stop blood flow to the brain by severing organs or arteries and veins. Or, with a direct shot to the head, the bullet can cause severe damage to the brain. In both instances, the game animal dies quickly with the least suffering.

The choice of a cartridge caliber and the type of bullet in the cartridge depend on the purpose for the gun. For target shooting, common choices are the round nose, semi-wadcutter and wadcutter bullets all of which are made of solid lead or the round nose copper jacketed bullets. Hunters make selections of ammunition based on the size of the game animal. For small game animals, such as rabbits and squirrels, a small caliber bullet that expands rapidly on impact is preferred because it does not penetrate deeply. For big game animals, such as deer, elk and moose, the hunter prefers a bullet that has a controlled release of energy upon impact, leading to greater penetration and damage to the animal's internal organs.

The bullet's depth and width of penetration in the target and its controlled expansion are important factors for self-defense purposes and for hunting. Manufacturers produce a wide variety of ammunition designed for hunting, target shooting, competitive shooting, home defense and personal defense.

Beyond the Target

The most common target stand for practicing pistol shooting skills is a hand made freestanding wooden frame with a large sheet of cardboard stapled onto the frame. The bulls eye target is stapled on the cardboard. When the pistol fires, the bullet passes through the target and comes to rest in a backstop down range. A solid backstop is necessary down range to end the bullet's flight. There must also be bullet-stopping material to the right and left sides of the target shooting area in the event that a bullet ricochets after striking the target frame or other solid material. When bullets strike a soft backstop, such as a mound of dirt, they will penetrate and come to rest in the dirt. Bullets shot onto the surface of water will skip over the water. When bullets strike hardwood, stones, steel or other solid objects, they bounce off the material (ricochet), and depending on the angle of impact, may fly in any direction, including straight back to the shooter or bystanders, causing severe injury, even death. A bullet ricochet is very dangerous.

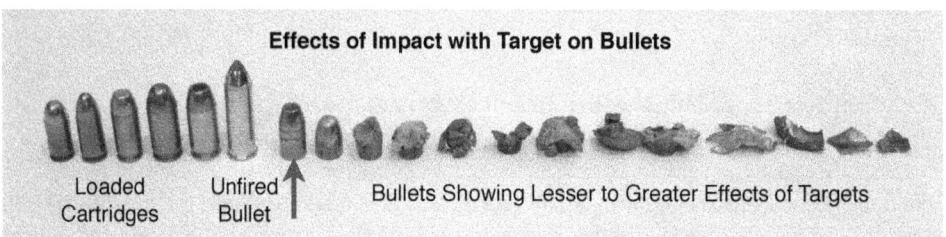

Never shoot into water or at solid objects.

Summary

This introduction to ballistics discussed the cartridge firing sequence. The first event is interior ballistics - what happens to the bullet from the instant the cartridge fires to when it exits the muzzle of the barrel. Exterior ballistics concerns the flight of the bullet once it leaves the muzzle until it reaches the target. Terminal ballistics defines the behavior of the bullet when it strikes the target and comes to rest either in the target or in something beyond the target. Shooters must be aware of the target and what lies beyond.

Quiz

1. The cartridge firing sequence begins when the firing pin strikes the primer.

    a. True

    b. False

2. The land of the rifling is the valley and the groove is the hill.

    a. True

    b. False

3. Ballistics is the study of the flight dynamics of projectiles.

   a. True

   b. False

4. Internal ballistics is the behavior of the bullet from the time the cartridge fires until the bullet exits the muzzle.

   a. True

   b. False

5. Exterior ballistics concerns what happens to the bullet when it first strikes the target and comes to rest.

   a. True

   b. False

6. Terminal ballistics concerns what happens during the flight of the bullet until it comes to rest in the target.

   a. True

   b. False

7. In what direction might a bullet travel after it strikes a solid object, such as hardwood, rock, or steel?

   a. An angle of ricochet to the right or left of the target

   b. An angle of ricochet upward and behind or in front of the target

   c. An angle of ricochet downward and behind or in front of the target

   d. All of the above

8. Shooting into a body of water, like a lake or stream, is safe because the bullet eventually comes to rest in the mud.

   a. True

   b. False

Chapter 8

Preparing for Live Fire

This chapter discusses initial steps to ensure that the shooting experience is safe and satisfying, including finding the dominant eye, gripping, dry firing, sight alignment and trigger squeeze, breath control, sight picture, recoil and follow-through. Plinking, target shooting, competitive shooting and hunting are some of the most enjoyable pursuits with handguns.

Training Ammunition Advisory

For the exercises in this chapter that involve a handgun, the beginner should use training ammunition or have no live ammunition in the gun until feeling safe and confident with the skill. After acquiring correct understanding, skill and confidence, load the gun with live ammunition to find out what happens when live firing at a target.

Dominant Eye

Determining eye dominance is an important step in preparation for shooting handguns. It is commonly known that people are either right-handed or left-handed. It is less well known that people have right eye or left eye dominance. Keeping both eyes open when pistol shooting is a good practice to follow, even though one eye is dominant.

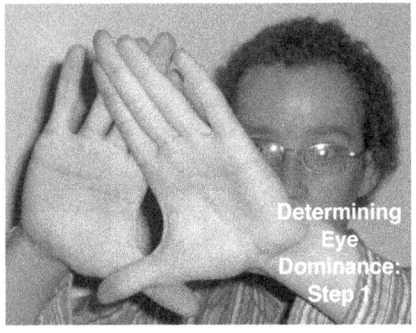

A shooter favors the dominant eye when shooting because it is stronger and does more work than the non-dominant eye. To determine which eye is dominant, complete this exercise. While facing a small object six to eight feet away, have both hands open but joined at the thumbs and facing away, with a small peep hole where the webs of the thumbs and forefingers intersect. Then, extend both arms fully and look through the hole at that small object with both eyes open.

While continuing to focus on the distant object, bring the hands back slowly to touch the face. The peephole should be over the dominant eye.

Alternatively, ask another person to help by standing six to eight feet in front. Repeat steps in this exercise, using the other person's nose as the object to focus on. The other person will be able to look through the peephole made by the shooter's hands and say which eye is dominant.

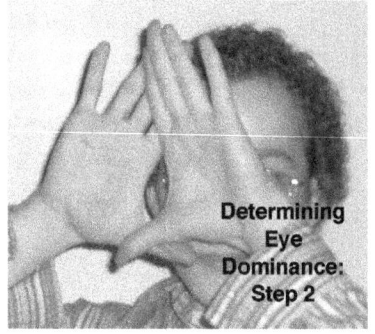

If a shooter is right-handed and right eye dominant, or left-handed and left eye dominant, it is relatively easy to obtain accurate shots on a target by holding the gun in the shooting hand and favoring the dominant eye when aiming and taking shots. Some shooters may prefer to close the non-dominant eye when shooting rather than keeping both eyes open. If doing so results in consistently accurate hits on the target that is a good practice to follow. Having both eyes open gives the shooter depth perception and greater peripheral vision.

A shooter with mixed dominance, which is right-handed but left eye dominant or left-handed and right eye dominant, or a person who has lost sight in the dominant eye on the same side as the shooting hand, may have to adjust shooting preferences to shoot accurately. Common solutions to mixed dominance for shooters are:

- Use the preferred shooting hand to hold the gun and put a piece of tape over the safety lens for the dominant eye, forcing the non-dominant eye to do all of the work with sighting, because it is on the same side of the body as the shooting hand.

🔵 Train the non-shooting hand for effective shooting skills and rely on the dominant eye for sighting, because it is on the same side of the body as the shooting hand.

Eye dominance is neither clear-cut nor forever. A person may have right eye dominance but in some situations the left eye takes over, or a person may be left eye dominant but at times the right eye takes control. As a person ages, eyesight may change, requiring a prescription for corrected vision. Eye dominance may change due to aging, injury or illness. If there are issues with vision, get an eye exam and seek a professional opinion from an optometrist.

Always wear eye protection and hearing protection when shooting.

Grip

The grip on a pistol is its handle. How to hold the pistol grip when shooting is also called the grip. Having a proper grip on a pistol is important for effective shooting.

One Hand and Two Hand Grip

Pointing a gun is like pointing with the index finger: the gun becomes an extension of the shooter's arm and hand, and takes the place of the index finger.

To understand the fundamentals of grip for pistol shooting, extend the shooting arm fully in front, with the hand at eye level. Point with the index finger to a distant object. Keep the other fingers and thumb closed in a fist and rotate the wrist so that the index finger is on top. Look directly over the index finger that is pointing at the distant object. This simple exercise demonstrates how to grip a pistol and aim at a target for one-handed shooting.

Taking Grip on Revolver

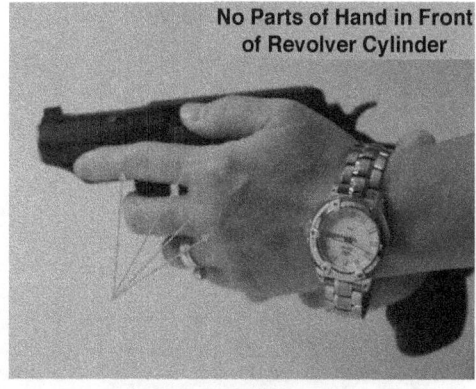

No Parts of Hand in Front of Revolver Cylinder

Taking this exercise one step farther, bring the non-shooting hand forward parallel with the extended shooting hand. The two arms will form a bow when the hands met. Wrap the fingers of the non-shooting hand around the fist of the shooting hand and position the thumb of the non-shooting hand over the thumb of the shooting hand. Look directly over the index finger that is pointing at the distant object. This basic exercise demonstrates the two hand grip, which provides greater control for pistol shooting than the one hand grip.

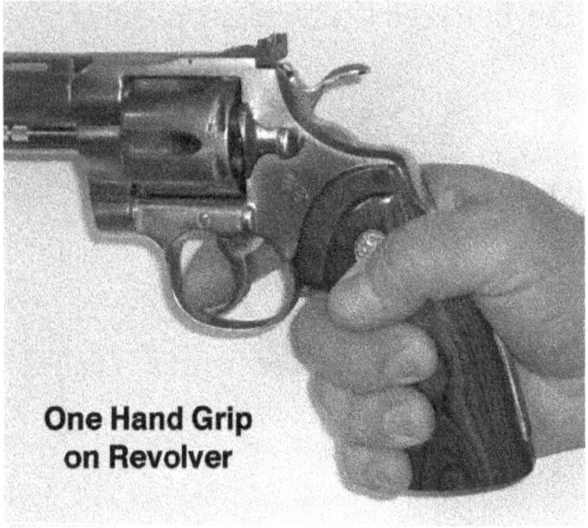

One Hand Grip on Revolver

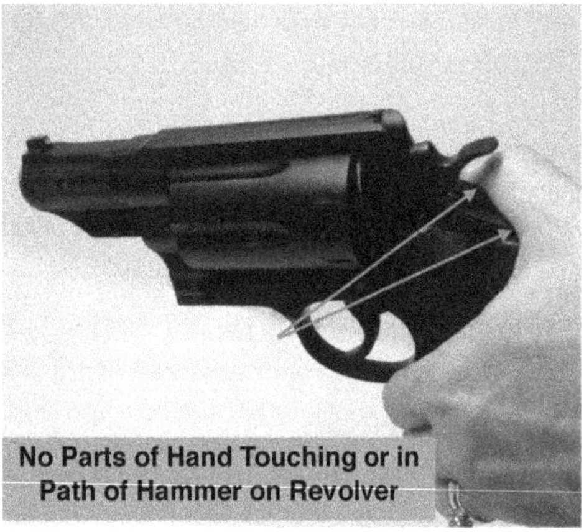

No Parts of Hand Touching or in Path of Hammer on Revolver

Obtaining a good grip on the pistol is important for maintaining control of the gun during shooting and for getting accurate shots on a target.

To develop a good pistol grip, follow these steps with an unloaded gun until the skill becomes routine.

- Keep the muzzle pointed in a safe direction, fingers off the trigger and fingers out of the trigger guard (ACTT).

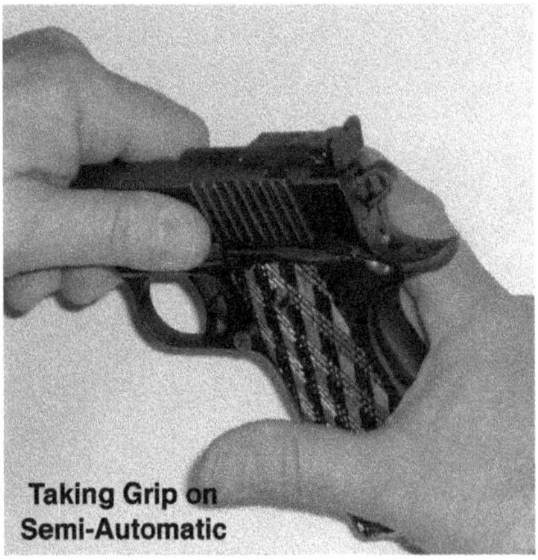

Taking Grip on Semi-Automatic

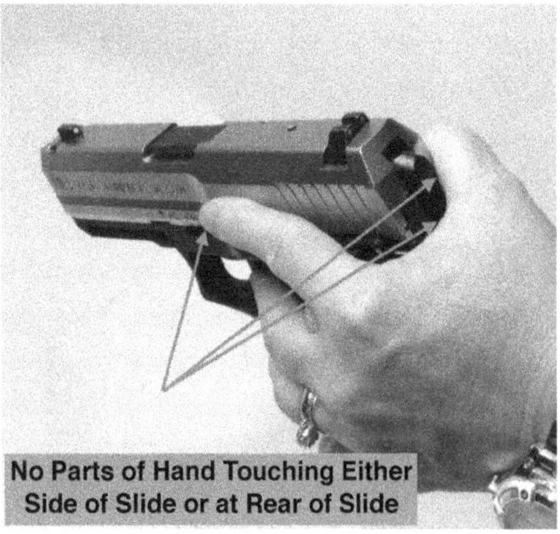

No Parts of Hand Touching Either Side of Slide or at Rear of Slide

One Hand Grip on Semi-Automatic

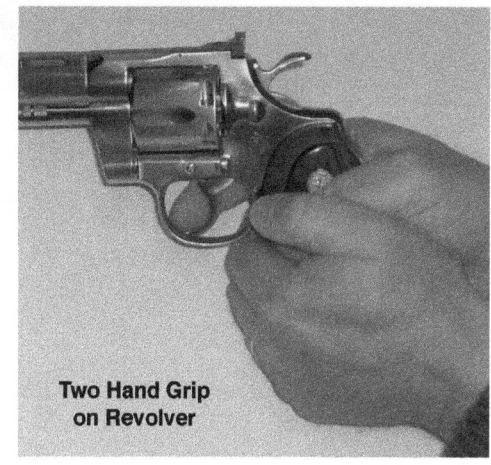
Two Hand Grip on Revolver

If the gun has a safety, keep it in the "ON" position. Use the non-shooting hand to pick up the gun by grasping the barrel or slide.

Two Hand Grip on Semi-Automatic Pistol

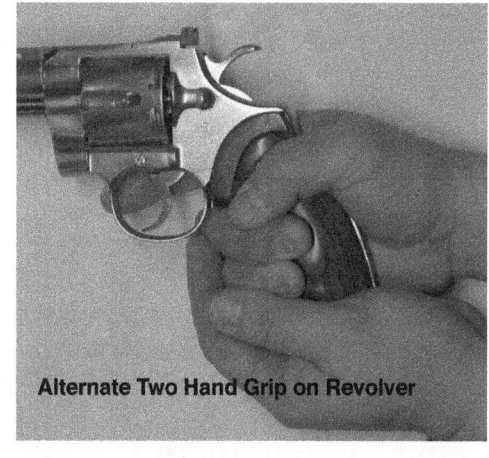
Alternate Two Hand Grip on Revolver

Alternate Two Hand Grip on Semi-Automatic Pistol

🔹 Place the gun's grip into the web of the shooting hand and close fingers around the grip for a firm, tight hold.

🔹 For revolvers, make certain that the web of the hand does not block the rearward movement of the hammer and that no fingers are in front of the chambers or touching the cylinder.

🔹 For semi-automatic pistols, make certain

that the web of the hand does not interfere with the rearward movement of the slide and that no fingers touch the slide.

- Examine the grip on the gun for a good feel and fit with the gun's grip, trigger and trigger guard.

- Adjust the grip as needed for control of the pistol and accuracy with shots.

- Point the gun and aim at a distant object, practicing both one-hand and two-hand grips.

For ordinary practice shooting events, use this same procedure to put the handgun in the shooting hand and use the same firm, tight grip.

When shooting a semi-automatic pistol, a firm, tight grip is necessary. A loose grip or too much flexing of the wrist at the instant of firing the cartridge may cause the action to jam.

If the pistol's grip feels too large or too small, it may be difficult to control the muzzle when a shot is taken. This creates a safety issue with control of the gun's recoil, and accuracy will be poor.

With the right-sized pistol grip, it should be easy to reach the trigger with the trigger finger for each shot. It should not be necessary to stretch the trigger finger to reach the trigger or force-fit a large finger into the trigger guard.

If the pistol grip does not fit the hand correctly, consider obtaining an after-market grip that fits your hand well, or determine if the manufacturer offers replacement grips for that gun to compensate for a smaller or larger shooting hand. Otherwise, acquire a handgun with a grip that fits your shooting hand properly.

Sight Alignment and Trigger Squeeze

Two important skills for a pistol shooter are sight alignment and trigger squeeze. For accurate shots, sight alignment and trigger squeeze must be done simultaneously.

The open sights on a pistol consist of a front sight that is a post and a rear sight that is a notch.

Sight alignment is correct aiming of the pistol - the front post must be in the center of the notch of the rear sight, with the tops of both even and in a straight line with the target.

Handgun Open Sights

To achieve correct sight alignment, begin by posting a target down range. Grip the pistol with the two hand position as if taking a shot. With the pistol pointed toward the target, place the top edge of front sight at the bottom edge of the bulls eye and at the same time place the front sight in the middle of the rear sight, with equal space on each side of the front sight and the top edges of both sights are even.

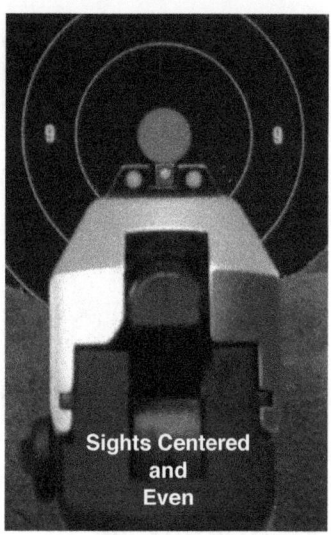

Sights Centered and Even

The eye can only focus on one thing at a time. Keep the eye focused on the front sight, but shift focus to check and see that the front sight remains positioned correctly in the center of the rear sight and its top stays at the bottom of the bulls eye.

This aiming of a pistol at the bulls eye target is called the 6 o'clock hold, and is preferred for practice and official bulls eye target shooting matches. Aiming at the center of a target is an option that is preferred for shooting at targets that do not have a clear marking for a dead center bulls eye, such as practice or competitive matches that use solid targets, such as falling steel plate targets, bowling pins or clay pigeons.

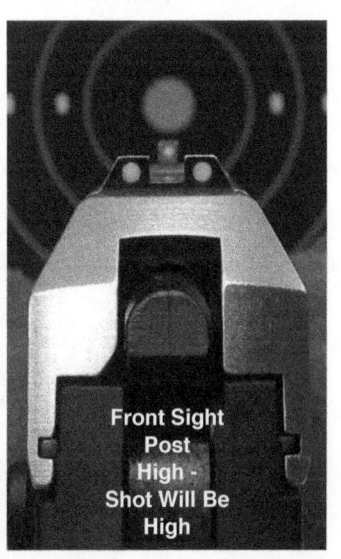

Front Sight Post High - Shot Will Be High

Trigger squeeze is gently, smoothly applying pressure on the trigger with the trigger finger - while holding the arm, wrist, and grip steady - until the gun fires. Correct trigger squeeze occurs if the gun fires when it "wants to" because of the continuous pressure on the trigger, and not when the shooter forces it to fire.

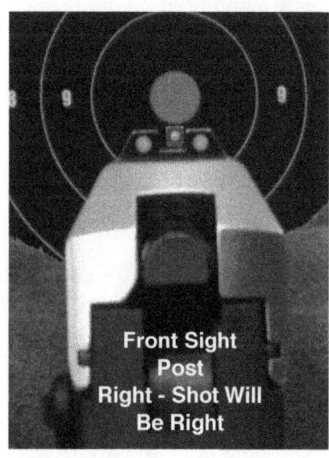

Front Sight Post Right - Shot Will Be Right

 Practice shooting to achieve correct, simultaneous sight alignment and trigger squeeze. The result will be consistent, accurate hits on the target.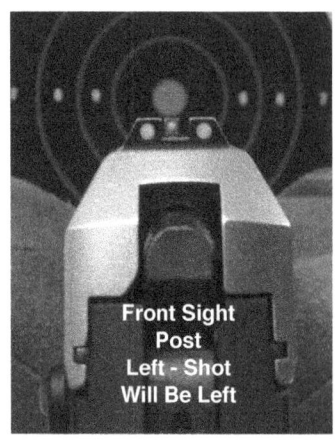

Sight Picture

The sight picture is what the shooter sees the instant the gun fires. Remembering the sight picture - the last place the sights pointed at before the gun fired - is important for analyzing a shot in preparation for the next shot.

Breath Control

While aiming the pistol at a target, take a deep breath, let out about three-quarters of the breath and hold it while gently squeezing the trigger until the gun fires. That is breath control.

Any movement of the gun that affects sight alignment will throw off the shot. The muzzle is the last thing that the bullet touches before it exits the bore. The slightest downward, upward or sideways movement of the gun will determine the final direction of travel for the bullet - an inaccurate shot.

Hold the gun with a steady grip, use breath control, align sights with the target and gently squeeze the trigger until the gun fires.

Dry Firing

Dry firing the handgun is an effective way to prepare for a shooting event and to improve accuracy.

Use training ammunition for this exercise and keep live ammunition stored safely away so there is no chance it may be used accidentally.

This exercise may be completed indoors, such as in a basement, or outdoors, including at a shooting range. Place a target out front. Take the standing position. Load the pistol with training ammunition.

For a revolver, choose either double action or single action. With either choice, the action will cycle until the exercise has ended.

For the semi-automatic pistol, operate the slide manually to load a training round in the chamber, cock the firing mechanism, squeeze the trigger and repeat operating the slide manually until the magazine is empty of training ammunition.

With a double action semi-automatic pistol, it is possible to cock the hammer manually and repeat squeezing the trigger on the same training cartridge. The training cartridge in the chamber will not eject when the trigger is squeezed, and cartridges in the magazine will not cycle into the chamber unless the slide is operated manually.

Practice dry firing the handgun with training ammunition. Concentrate on lining up the sights with the target and squeezing the trigger. Develop the habit of remembering where the muzzle of the gun was pointed the instant that the gun "fired." Also concentrate on sight alignment and trigger squeeze during live firing exercises. By alternating this technique between dry firing and live firing practice sessions, a shooter will eventually be able to accurately guess where the bullets hit the target. Dry firing is an inexpensive and effective way to develop pistol shooting accuracy.

Recoil

When the cartridge fires in a pistol, the pressure from the shot forces the shooter's hand and arm to the rear and also upward. All cartridges produce recoil when fired. The extent of recoil varies from little to great, depending on the caliber and gunpowder load for the cartridge. The overall weight of the gun and the length of the gun barrel also affect felt recoil. Generally, a heavy gun with a long barrel produces less recoil. Firing a .22 caliber pistol with a standard load results in slight recoil, whereas firing a .44 Magnum pistol creates significant recoil.

It is not possible to stop recoil, but a skillful pistol shooter can control recoil with the correct, constantly held grip and by allowing only slight flexing of the wrist and upward movement of the arm at the instant the gun fires.

Begin development of pistol shooting skills by practicing with a small caliber gun - the .22 caliber cartridge is the best choice. This ammunition is generally low cost, the recoil is slight and the cartridge is accurate to 50 yards and more.

Starting the sport of pistol shooting with a large caliber gun may create bad physical and psychological habits that can be difficult to unlearn, due to the significant recoil and loud blast when the gun fires. Firing a big gun can also be a serious safety issue if the shooter does not have the skills to handle the gun's recoil.

Build good pistol shooting skills over time, by starting with a small caliber gun and changing up to larger calibers when ready.

Always wear eye protection and hearing protection when shooting.

Follow Through

Follow through is completing everything for the shot correctly: before the cartridge fires, when the cartridge fires and after the cartridge fires.

At the instant the cartridge fires, the shooter feels the recoil of the shot and responds to the recoil before taking the next shot. Recoil varies from slight to great, depending on the cartridge and the size and weight of the gun. Heavy recoil may affect follow through significantly.

Develop good follow through with the following exercise.

- Before the shot: align the sights with target and gently squeeze the trigger until the gun fires.

- During the shot: maintain sight alignment and trigger squeeze; remember the sight picture and control recoil.

- After the shot: analyze sight picture for the completed shot and realign sights for the next shot.

What the shooter does at the instant the cartridge fires is follow through. Correct follow through is the mark of a skillful shooter.

Summary

Preparation for live firing ensures safe and accurate pistol shooting. The uppermost concern is to follow the fundamental firearm safety rules (ACTT) at all times when handling guns. A beginning shooter should use training ammunition until the routines are safe, familiar and effective.

This chapter described specific skills for shooting revolvers and semi-automatic pistols, including determining the dominant eye, gripping the pistol, one-handed and two-handed grips, dry firing, sight alignment and trigger squeeze, sight picture, breath control, recoil and follow through. Ongoing practice will build confidence with these skills in preparation for life fire with revolvers and pistols and help achieve accurate results on the target.

Quiz

1. The dominant eye is stronger and does more work than the non-dominant eye.

    a. True

    b. False

2. Dry firing a pistol is a technique where the shooter sets up a target and practices sight alignment and trigger squeeze without using live ammunition.

    a. True

    b. False

3. Proper sight alignment is having the front sight post evenly spaced in the notch of the rear sight with the tops of both sights even.

    a. True

    b. False

4. For the grip on a revolver, never have fingers in front of the cylinder and keep the web of the hand away from the rear of the hammer.

    a. True

    b. False

5. For the grip of a semi-automatic pistol, never allow fingers to touch the slide, but having the web of the shooting hand behind the slide is not an issue.

   a. True

   b. False

6. Gripping the handgun with one hand gives greater control of the gun during firing.

   a. True

   b. False

7. Breath control involves taking a deep breath before aiming the handgun and holding it until the gun fires.

   a. True

   b. False

8. Follow through involves taking correct steps before, during and after the cartridge fires.

   a. True

   b. False

Chapter 9

Taking First Shots

This chapter describes basic pistol shooting positions, how to take safe and skillful first shots and how to adjust sights for consistent, accurate hits on a target. Accurate pistol shooting is an acquired skill that takes many hours of practice.

Training Ammunition Advisory

For the exercises in this chapter that involve a handgun, the beginner should use training ammunition or have no live ammunition in the gun until feeling safe and confident with the skill. After acquiring correct understanding, skill and confidence, load the gun with live ammunition to find out what happens when shooting at a target.

For the first experience with shooting a handgun, obtain guidance from a NRA certified instructor or someone with substantial practical knowledge of handguns.

Basic Shooting Positions

This discussion of basic shooting positions includes sitting or bench rest shooting, one hand shooting and two hand shooting. The purpose for a formal shooting event may determine the pistol shooting positions.

For some official pistol matches, shooters may be required to use only the standing, one hand position for all courses of fire. For other official pistol shooting events, the one hand or the two hand position may be required, or both the one hand and the two hand positions may be required, or both shooting positions may be optional.

For ordinary practice sessions, the shooter selects any shooting position, but should develop skill with each of these positions because each one serves an important purpose.

Sitting or Bench Rest Position

At the firing line on most pistol shooting ranges, there is a bench that a shooter may sit at for pistol shooting. Using a bench rest helps to control the handgun, allowing as little human error as possible. Bench rest shooting is a good choice to determine where the bullet strikes the target.

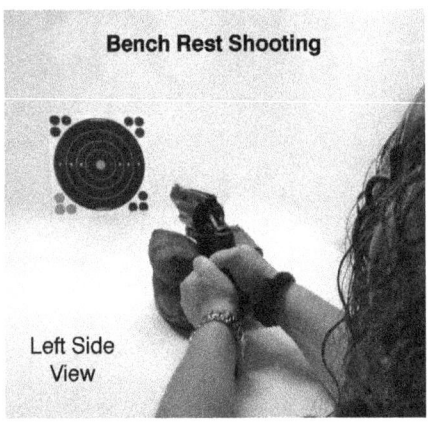

Bench Rest Shooting
Left Side View

The shooter may use the bench rest with elbows positioned on the bench top to steady the gun for each shot. Or use a gun rest, such as a bag filled with sand, on the bench as a prop to control gun movement. Or use a gun vise on the bench to provide maximum control for each shot.

If a shooter has had little or no experience with a large caliber cartridge, the bench rest position provides control of the firearm to determine the extent of recoil for the first live firing of the big gun. Bench rest shooting is a good choice for the beginning shooter who may be unfamiliar with handguns or afraid of the gun's firing and recoil. Long distance bench rest shooting may be the preferred choice for hunting with a handgun or for competition.

Practice bench rest shooting with training ammunition or with no ammunition in the gun until ready to take the first shot. When the shooting range is clear, post a bulls eye target down range and return to the shooting line. If the range is safe, prepare for live fire and follow these steps.

  Keep the muzzle pointed in a safe direction, fingers off the trigger and fingers out of the trigger guard (ACTT).

- Load the pistol. If the gun is equipped with a safety, keep it "ON" until ready to fire a shot.

- Place the pistol on the rest.

- Grip the pistol as explained in the section on grip. Rest the trigger finger on the gun's frame just above the trigger guard.

- Obtain correct sight-alignment with the target.

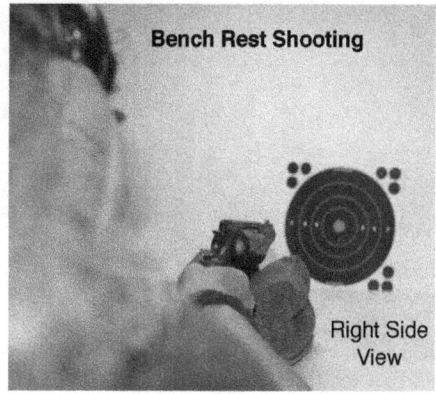

Bench Rest Shooting

Right Side View

- For single action shooting, use the thumb on the non-shooting hand to cock the hammer or action. Squeeze the trigger to fire the gun. Trigger squeeze will be light.

- For double action shooting, squeeze the trigger to fire the gun. There is no additional step to cock the hammer or action. Trigger squeeze will be hard.

- Repeat firing as desired.

- Open the gun's action, remove all spent cases and loaded cartridges or the magazine. Keep the gun unloaded, action open, safety "ON," if so equipped and the chamber visible for inspection.

Check where the shots hit the target by using a spotting scope or binoculars. After achieving a tight group by firing the handgun on a bench rest, the shooter may adjust the gun's sights for consistent, bulls eye hits on the target.

When the shooting range is clear, retrieve the target or post a new target.

Standing Two Hand Position

The standing two hand shooting position provides the shooter with the most control of the handgun for off-hand shooting. This next exercise is a follow-up to the section in Chapter 8 concerning "One Hand and Two Hand Grip." This exercise develops skill with one method of gripping the pistol for the standing, two

Practicing Two Hand Grip

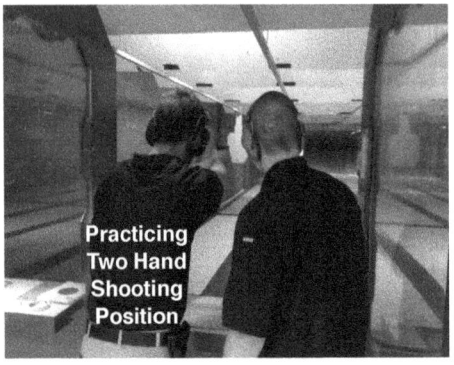

hand shooting position and for the standing, one hand position.

To prepare for and complete the live firing event with the standing, two hand position, follow these steps outlined for shooting revolvers and semi-automatic pistols.

Revolvers

When the shooting range is clear, post a bulls eye target downrange. Return to the shooting line for live firing.

If there are any concerns about confidence or safety for taking the first shots with a handgun, begin with training ammunition and then switch to live ammunition when ready.

Follow these steps.

- Keep the muzzle pointed in a safe direction, fingers off the trigger and fingers out of the trigger guard (ACTT).

- Grip the revolver.

- Load the revolver.

- Rest the trigger finger on the revolver's frame just above the trigger guard.

- Raise the revolver with both arms to aim at the target.

- For single action revolver shooting, use the thumb of the non-shooting hand to cock the hammer and then return this thumb to its position on top of the other thumb. Trigger squeeze will be light.

- For double action revolver shooting, continue to grip the gun with both hands. There is no separate step to cock the hammer with a thumb. Trigger squeeze will be hard.

- When ready to take the first shot, obtain correct sight-alignment with the target and move the trigger finger into the trigger guard until it gently rests on the trigger.

- Squeeze the trigger steadily until the revolver fires.

- Remove the finger from the trigger guard and rest it on the revolver's frame.

- For follow-up shots, repeat this sequence.

After achieving confidence with single action revolver shooting, adjust the practice of repeat shooting in single action as follows. Continue with the same grip, but keep the thumb of the non-shooting hand raised and not touching the frame or hammer. In this position, this thumb continues cocking of the hammer for repeat firing of the revolver until all cartridges have fired.

Between courses of live firing, open the revolver's action, remove all spent cases and live ammunition. Place the revolver with the cylinder open on top of the shooting bench for easy inspection of the chambers. Use a spotting scope or binoculars to determine where the shots hit the target. Continue practicing until achieving a tight group.

Do not go down range to post or retrieve targets until the shooting line is clear.

Semi-Automatic Pistols

- Keep the muzzle pointed in a safe direction, fingers off the trigger and fingers out of the trigger guard (ACTT).

- Load the magazine.

- Grip the semi-automatic pistol. Adjust the position of the shooting-hand thumb to operate the safety, and put the safety in the "ON" position, if so equipped.

- Rest the trigger finger on the pistol's frame just above the trigger guard.

- With the non-shooting hand, pull back the slide and lock it into position with the slide stop.

- Put the magazine into the magazine well and push hard until it clicks into place.

- Raise the pistol with both arms to aim at the target.

- Release the slide by operating the slide release. Put the safety in the "OFF" position, if so equipped. The pistol is ready to fire.

- For single action shooting, trigger squeeze will be light.

- For double action shooting, trigger squeeze will be hard.

- When ready to take the first shot, obtain correct sight-alignment with the target and move the trigger finger into the trigger guard until it gently rests on the trigger.

- Squeeze the trigger steadily until the pistol fires.

- Remove the finger from the trigger guard and rest it on the pistol's frame.

- For follow-up shots, repeat this sequence.

After achieving confidence with single action and double action pistol shooting, keep the trigger finger inside the trigger guard for a more rapid course of fire with the auto-loading pistol. If there is any reason to pause or interrupt shooting, immediately take the trigger finger out of the trigger guard and rest it on the frame.

Between courses of live fire, bring the gun down from the shooting position, put the safety "ON," if so equipped, remove the magazine, and operate the slide to open the action to eject the cartridge, and lock the slide to the rear. Place the pistol on the shooting bench with the opening to the chamber facing up and the safety showing "ON," if so equipped.

Use a spotting scope or binoculars to determine where the shots hit the target. Continue practicing until achieving a tight group.

Do not go downrange to post or retrieve targets until the shooting line is clear.

Standing One Hand Position

The standing, one hand position is an option that every pistol shooter should practice until capable of getting consistent, accurate hits on a target. It is a more challenging pistol shooting position for all types of shooting practice or competitions and also for defensive use because only one hand grips and fires the gun.

If a shooter is developing handgun shooting skills for personal defense, competency with the standing, one hand shooting position is necessary in the event that the non-shooting arm is disabled. Also, to fully develop skills for personal defense with a handgun, the shooter should practice shooting with the non-shooting arm.

To prepare for and complete live fire with the standing, one hand position, follow these steps for shooting revolvers and semi-automatic pistols.

Revolvers and Semi-Automatic Pistols

Practicing One Hand Shooting Position

- Keep the muzzle pointed in a safe direction, fingers off the trigger and fingers out of the trigger guard (ACTT).

- Follow the same steps as outlined above for standing, two hand shooting with revolvers and semi-automatic pistols.

- During courses of fire, have the non-shooting arm hanging loose at the side of the body, or put that hand in the jacket or pants pocket.

For the revolver, a significant amount of practice may be necessary to become proficient with operating the hammer with the thumb of the shooting hand to cock the revolver for single-action shooting. If confidence is lacking, begin developing this skill with training ammunition. Alternatively, use the non-shooting thumb to cock the hammer between shots by raising and lowering that arm between shots.

For the semi-automatic pistol, use the non-shooting hand to release the slide and put the safety in the "OFF" position, if so equipped.

Shooting from the standing, one hand position with a double action revolver or semi-automatic pistol is challenging and requires practice to become accurate.

Adjusting Sights

The sights on a pistol help a shooter aim at the target and make accurate shots. The common kinds of sights for pistols are open sights (also called iron sights), telescopic sights, red dot sights, laser sights and holographic sights. This discussion will concern adjustment of open sights because they are simple to use and dependable

Pistols for personal or home defense and police and military use are intended for very close use and may have the simplest of open sight systems: a fixed post as the front sight and a notch cut in the frame for the rear sight. These sights are not adjustable. The gun is ready to shoot.

Pistols for accurate defensive use, target shooting, hunting and competitive shooting are designed for shooting at targets at greater distances where accurate shooting is a concern, and these guns will have an adjustable rear sight or both the front and rear sights are adjustable. Consult the owner's manual from the manufacturer for more specific steps to adjust the gun's sights.

The basic objective for this target shooting practice session is to have a consistent and reasonably tight group in the center of a bulls eye target.

After taking a dozen or more shots at a bulls eye target set at 10 to 15 yards downrange, analyze the target to determine how spread out the hits are from one another and what is the approximate center of all the hits. If the spread of hits appears to be more or less random, with some hits way out of the center, post new targets, closer if need be, and practice to develop shooting skills to achieve hits on the targets that fall consistently closer together someplace on the target before adjusting the sights.

When the hits on the target consistently fall together in a group, even a loose group, and are clustering around the center, continue practice sessions to tighten the group in the bulls eye. It may not be necessary to adjust the sights.

If the hits form a loose group but are not clustering around the center of the target, prepare to adjust the rear sight. Study the hits to determine the approximate center of all hits. Use a highlighting marker to mark that spot on the target. Determine where this average center of the hits is at in relation to the X-ring of the bulls eye - the center of the target. To adjust open sights, the simple rule is to move the rear sight in the same direction that the shot group should move in order to have the shots hit the center of the bulls eye target.

Open Sights
Windage Adjustment

Turn Screw to Move Sight In Same Direction to Move Hits on Target

Open Sights
Elevation Adjustment

Turn Screw to Move Sight In Same Direction to Move Hits on Target

Adjusting the rear sight on a pistol is a one or a two step process. When adjusting sights, make one adjustment at a time. Repeat practice shooting. Change the target as needed. Then, repeat firing at the target with each successive adjustment of the sights until the shot group is hitting the X-ring consistently.

Sight adjustment is a one step process if the shot group is on a horizontal line with the bulls eye, but to the left, for example. Adjust the rear sight to the right where the shots should go to hit the bulls eye. Adjust the rear sight to the left, if the shot group is on a horizontal line, but to the right of the bulls eye. If the shot group is on a vertical line with the bulls eye, but high or low, adjust the rear sight down or up to move the shot group to hit the bulls eye.

Sight adjustment is a two step process if the shot group is in either of the quadrants of the target. Move the rear sight in the same direction that the shot group should move, but only one direction at a time. For the high and right side shot group, adjust the rear sight down. Repeat firing until the shot group is in a horizontal line with the bulls eye. Then, adjust the rear sight to the left. Repeat firing until the shot group is in the bulls eye. Follow the same logical movement of the rear sight for shot groups in the other quadrants.

Adjusting the front sight is not commonly done. If the gun is equipped with an adjustable front sight and it must be adjusted, its movement is always opposite to where the shots must move to hit the bulls eye.

Summary

This chapter presented a discussion of skills and recommended practice sessions to help the beginning pistol shooter get on target and achieve accuracy with revolvers and semi-automatic pistols. Topics included the bench rest shooting position, standing two hand shooting position, standing one hand shooting position and how to adjust open sights.

Quiz

1. What shooting position should be used when unsure of the recoil or accuracy of a handgun?

    a. Two hand

    b. Bench rest

    c. One hand

2. A key factor in the one hand and two hand shooting positions is control of the handgun.

    a. True

    b. False

3. What should be done if there is concern about one's ability to load, fire and unload a handgun?

    a. Practice with standard loads

    b. Practice with +P loads

    c. Practice with training ammunition

    d. Practice with +P+ loads

4. When adjusting open sights, move the rear sight in the same direction that the hits should move on the target.

    a. True

    b. False

Chapter 10

Cleaning Handguns

The purpose for cleaning a handgun after a shooting session is to restore it to good operating condition for dependable, subsequent use. If guns are in storage for long periods, they should be cleaned and lubricated on a regular basis. If the purpose of the handgun is to provide personal protection, it should be inspected, cleaned and lubricated on a more frequent schedule.

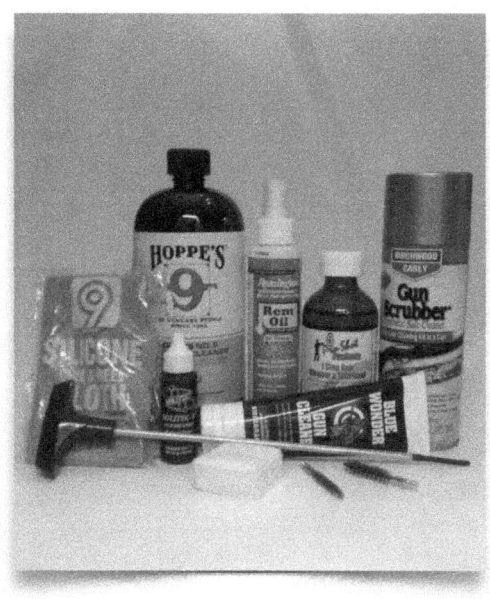

Handgun Cleaning Essentials

When a cartridge fires in a handgun, it leaves carbon fouling from the burned gunpowder throughout the action and bore, and carbon, lead, and copper fouling in the bore. Depending on the circumstances at an outdoor shooting range, there may be dirt and water in the gun. When a handgun is stored over a long period, lubricants and protective coatings may evaporate, leaving the gun's action and exterior surface dry.

A dirty or dry handgun can fail to operate as designed. Firing a dirty gun can damage the gun and cause injury to the shooter. The handgun cleaning process should remove fouling and grime from all parts of the gun, lubricate moving parts and apply a thin protective coating to internal and external surfaces to prevent corrosion.

Gun Cleaning Safety Rules

Follow these safety rules when cleaning guns.

- Keep the muzzle pointed in a safe direction, fingers off the trigger and fingers out of the trigger guard (ACTT).

- Unload guns before cleaning.

- Remove all ammunition from the work area.

- Clean guns as soon as possible after each use. Clean guns periodically if stored for long periods.

- Use training ammunition to check the operation of the gun's action.

Tools, Solvents and Preservatives

The basic tools and materials for a handgun cleaning kit include:

- Cleaning rod sized for a pistol.

- Cleaning patches sized for the gun's bore.

- Bore cleaning brushes sized for the gun's bore.

- Small nylon brush and cotton swabs to remove dirt and residue.

- Gun bore inspection light.

- Soft rag coated with preservative to wipe down parts and the gun's exterior surface.

There are many products available for cleaning handguns, some are synthetic and others are petroleum-based. The most versatile cleaning products are designed to accomplish all three gun cleaning purposes at once: penetrate and clean fouling, dirt and grime from metal surfaces, lubricate moving parts to reduce friction, and protect the metal surfaces from moisture and other corrosive substances.

There are also gun cleaning products that are designed to remove a significant buildup of powder, lead, plastic and copper fouling. In the event of heavy buildup, the multi-purpose cleaning solvent may not be sufficient for a thorough cleaning. Use a specially formulated bore cleaning product to remove an excessive buildup of fouling.

Gun Cleaning Oils and Solvents

Handgun Cleaning Process

The first step: follow the gun cleaning safety rules.

The cleaning process for revolvers is different from the cleaning process for semi-automatic pistols.

Study the owner's manual from the manufacturer to know the parts and features of the gun, how the action operates, disassembly, correct cleaning process, where to apply lubrication and reassembly.

Gun Cleaning Materials and Process for Revolver

Do not disassemble a revolver.

Disassemble a semi-automatic pistol only to the extent that the manufacturer recommends in the owner's manual.

Clean the handgun in a well-ventilated area that is set up for cleaning guns. Consider wearing protective gloves and safety glasses to prevent direct contact with hazardous and toxic gun cleaning chemicals. Place a plastic sheet or a gun cleaning mat on the surface of a bench or table and cover it with an absorbent material, such as newspaper, shop towel or rag.

Gun Cleaning Materials and Process for Semi-Automatic

The most difficult part of the gun cleaning process is removing copper, lead or plastic fouling from the gun's bore.

Steps for Cleaning Handguns

☻ Open the action, make certain the handgun is unloaded and remove all ammunition from the work area.

☻ For revolvers: with the action open, inspect the cylinder and chambers for overall condition.

☻ For semi-automatic pistols: with the action open, remove the magazine and disassemble the pistol. Inspect all parts for overall condition.

☻ Attach the correct bore cleaning brush to the cleaning rod and apply cleaning solvent to the brush.

☻ Grasp the barrel and brace it on the bench while running the cleaning brush back and forth several times to scrub the bore; do the same for all chambers of a revolver.

☻ Attach a dry cleaning patch to the cleaning rod with a patch holder and run this through the bore and chambers. Inspect the patch. Replace the dirty patch with a clean one and repeat the process several times.

☻ Use a bore inspection light or flashlight to inspect the bore and chambers. If the interior surface is dull gray (powder, lead or plastic fouling) or shiny gold (copper fouling), repeat cleaning with a wet bore brush dipped in a specialty cleaning solvent for removing lead, plastic and copper. Scrub repeatedly with the wet bore brush.

☻ Alternate use of a dry cleaning patch with a wet bore brush in the bore and chambers until a dry cleaning patch comes out clean.

☻ Attach a cleaning patch moistened with gun oil or preservative and pass this through the bore and chambers to leave a thin layer to protect these interior surfaces from moisture.

☻ Use the nylon brush, cotton swabs and gun cleaning solvent to remove debris and fouling from all areas of the gun, including for the revolver: the cylinder, cartridge ejector rod and star; and for the semi-automatic pistol: the guide spring and rod, feed ramp, slide rails on the frame and slide, magazine well. Wipe surfaces with a clean rag moistened with gun oil.

☻ Apply gun oil to all parts where recommended in the owner's manual.

☻ Wipe down all exterior surfaces with a rag moistened with gun oil or preservative.

☻ Close the action on the revolver. Reassemble the semi-automatic pistol and reinsert the empty magazine. Determine that the action operates correctly for the revolver and semi-automatic pistol.

☻ Return the handgun to secure storage.

Summary

Clean the gun as soon as possible after use and periodically, if the gun is stored unused for long periods of time. A dirty or dry firearm may not operate safely. During firing a dirty gun may cause damage to the gun or injure the shooter or bystanders.

The gun is always loaded; treat the gun safely by following the fundamental firearm safety rules when cleaning - ACTT.

Before starting the cleaning process, consult the owner's manual from the manufacturer to become familiar with the gun's parts, features, action, cleaning process and where to apply lubrication.

Revolvers do not require disassembly for cleaning, only opening of the action. Semi-automatic pistols require disassembly for cleaning. Follow the manufacturer's instructions to disassemble and reassemble the pistol.

Cleaning the gun's bore until it is free of carbon, lead, copper or plastic fouling is the most difficult task. There are many different varieties of gun cleaning products on the market. Some are multi-functional, including cleaning, lubricating and protecting the gun, and others are designed to remove the worst cases of fouling in the gun's bore.

A handgun cleaning kit should include an assortment of tools, solvents and oils to clean all parts of the handgun.

After cleaning the handgun, check to see that the action operates correctly using training ammunition.

Return the handgun to secure storage.

Quiz

1. When should the handgun be cleaned?

    a. As soon as possible after use

    b. Never, smokeless powder is clean burning

    c. When the gun misfires or jams

2. What should not be present when cleaning a gun?

    a. Instruction manual

    b. Newspaper

    c. Ammunition

3. What step must be taken to clean the semi-automatic pistol that is different from cleaning the revolver?

    a. Disassemble the pistol

    b. Read the instruction manual

    c. Use specialized solvents

Chapter 11

Storing Handguns

The owner of firearms and ammunition is responsible for their secure storage. State laws govern storage of firearms and ammunition. Store all firearms securely so they are not accessible by unauthorized persons, especially children. There are gun locks that may be applied to the action or trigger and storage devices for guns and ammunition, including cabinets, cases, vaults and safes.

Security and Use

The handgun's purpose - personal, business or home defense, target or competitive shooting, hunting and collecting - will influence the owner's decision about what type of security system to use. Handgun security systems help to ensure safe storage. Yet, if the handgun is intended for immediate use, as in personal, business or home defense, and the key or tool is missing or the battery is dead, the gun storage system cannot be unlocked for use.

Unless the firearm must be available for immediate defense, it should be stored unloaded, locked up. Ammunition should be stored separate from firearms in a locked container.

A gun lock or storage device is not foolproof. Anything manmade can fail. Gun security devices are designed to help prevent unauthorized access, but there is no perfect security system. The gun owner's vigilance is the best gun security backup system.

Action Locks and Trigger Locks

Guns may be secured with after-market gun locks, and also gun manufacturers have designed handguns with built-in security systems.

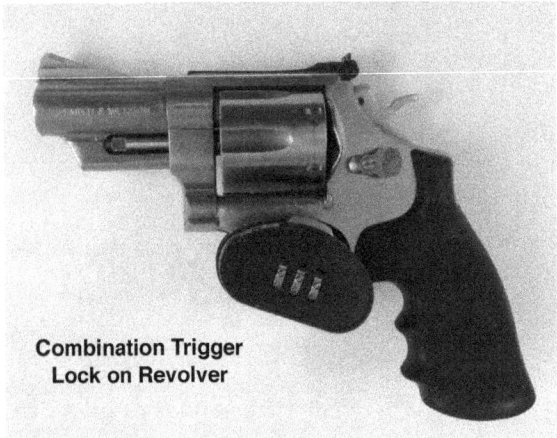

Combination Trigger Lock on Revolver

There are two-piece trigger locks, using a key or combination locks, that are forced together from opposite sides of the trigger guard to prevent access to the trigger.

Another type is a mechanical, key-activated action lock. Once locked with the key, the gun's action will not operate unless it is unlocked with the key. Another type is an electronic lock that uses a fingerprint recognition system to lock and unlock the gun's action.

Cable Lock on Semi-Automatic

Action Lock on Semi-Automatic

There are action locks that employ a cable and padlock to wrap through the action to prevent the gun's use. Another type uses a breech or bore locking device to prevent opening the gun's action.

Cabinets and Cases

Gun storage cabinets provide safe storage for a collection of firearms. These cabinets may be made of sheet steel with a hinged door that is locked with a key. There are also gun cabinets made of wood and glass with locking doors, drawers and and storage bins. Usually, the gun cabinets made of wood and glass are designed to be showcases, and the room where they are located may have additional security systems to prevent unauthorized access.

There are many different kinds of small cases for one or two handguns. Typically, these cases are made of heavy duty metal or plastic, with latches that snap shut and are lockable or have tabs for applying padlocks to prevent access.

Vaults and Safes

Handgun security vaults are made of heavy-duty steel and are designed to store one or two handguns with magazines, cartridge loading devices and spare ammunition. They provide secure access with a variety of mechanical and electronic locking systems, including keys, combination locks, finger pressure, and fingerprint recognition. These gun storage systems are mini-safes, which may be mounted on furniture or inside a vehicle for personal, business or home defense.

A gun safe is the most secure storage system for firearms. Gun safes vary in size from relatively small for storing several firearms to room-sized for a large firearm collection. Access to a gun safe may involve one or more mechanisms, including a key, mechanical combination or electronic combination lock. The walls, roof, bottom and door of a gun safe are made of thick steel and the door employs a series of locking bolts around the entire perimeter to secure the door. These heavy-duty gun safes may also have ratings for fire protection.

Summary

The gun owner is responsible for safe storage of the firearm - safe from access by unauthorized persons, especially children. Stay up-to-date on applicable state laws pertaining to storage of firearms and ammunition. There are various gun locks, cabinets, cases, vaults and safes for securing firearms. The gun owner should employ one or more of these systems to ensure safe storage. But there is no perfect system. The gun owner must safeguard guns and ammunition from unauthorized access.

Quiz

1. The owner is not responsible for safe storage of firearms.

    a. True

    b. False

2. What is considered to be the safest means to store firearms when not in use?

    a. Trigger lock

    b. Cable lock

    c. Gun safe

    d. Metal cabinet

3. What is the best means of safeguarding guns and ammunition from unauthorized persons.

   a. Locking cabinet

   b. Gun vault

   c. Gun safe

   d. Gun owner's constant vigilance

Chapter 12

Next Steps

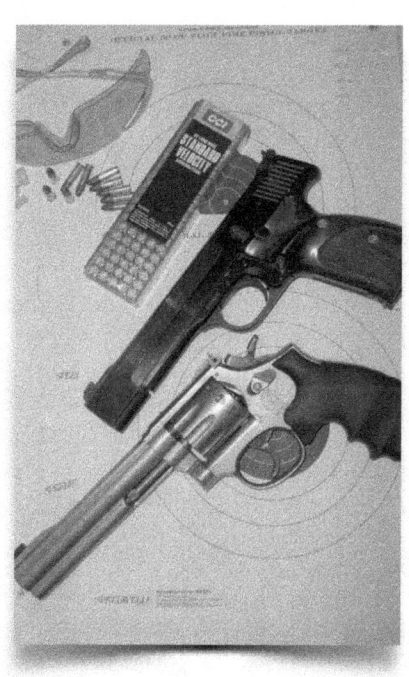

This chapter explains what a beginning pistol owner should do to develop a basic level of proficiency with shooting a handgun at bulls eye targets. The gun is always loaded. Handle all guns safely by following the fundamental firearm safety rules - ACTT.

Reasons for Handgun Ownership

The reasons for owning a handgun may include one or more of the following: personal defense, business defense, home defense, target shooting, plinking, hunting, competitive shooting and collecting. If the purpose is only to collect handguns, not to use them, then the owner stores them securely and maintains them periodically over time.

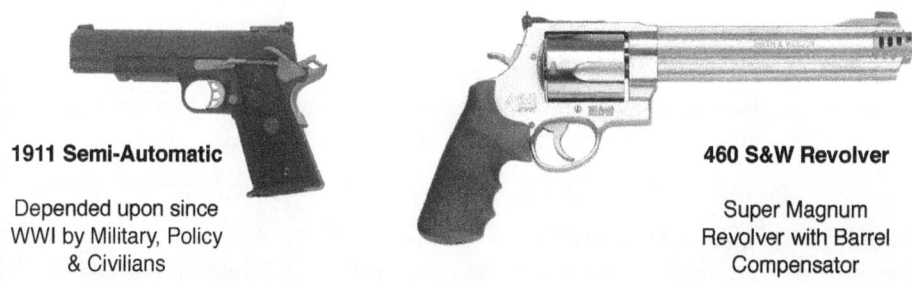

1911 Semi-Automatic

Depended upon since
WWI by Military, Policy
& Civilians

460 S&W Revolver

Super Magnum
Revolver with Barrel
Compensator

If the purpose for owning a handgun is to use it, the owner should become familiar with the gun's features, how the gun operates, and develop skills for safe and accurate shooting.

Practice

Pistol shooting practice is the sporting use of handguns. Periodic, sustained pistol shooting practice develops familiarity with the handgun, knowledge and skill with safe handling and leads to accurate shots on a target. Practice of pistol shooting skills develops proficiency - it is challenging and fun.

Two things are important for developing pistol shooting proficiency: access to a proper shooting range and guidance from a certified pistol instructor or a pistol shooter with greater experience. Unless the handgun owner has the land, backstop and related facilities for a pistol range, it is best to join a sportsmen's club that has a pistol range. Membership in a sportsmen's club may lead to participation in a pistol league and guidance from new found friends who are experts or certified instructors. Handgun shooting lessons are available for a fee from certified instructors and professional pistol training companies.

The best choice to develop good pistol shooting skills is bulls eye target shooting. The shooting range at a sportsmen's club may have rules for how close to the firing line targets may be posted. If permitted, the beginning shooter first sets up a bulls eye target down range at 10 yards to 15 yards. If the handgun has adjustable sights, make adjustments as needed to get the hits in the X-ring consistently. Then, practice for greater proficiency with the target set at 25 yards and 50 yards.

Handgun shooting activities vary from informal basic bulls eye target shooting to elaborate defensive shooting scenarios and Olympic Games. Formal pistol shooting events have rules for various aspects of the event, including the kind of handguns to use, ammunition, targets, shooting positions, courses of fire, range activity and target scoring. There are indoor and outdoor handgun shooting ranges for practice and competition. Consult the section below on "Resources for Self-Help" for additional details.

Analyze Targets

When shooting a handgun, focus on the front sight, align the front and rear sights on the bulls eye of the target, acquire the sight picture, and gently squeeze the trigger until the gun fires.

Knowing how to place the trigger finger on the trigger and how to squeeze the trigger directly to the rear, while maintaining sight alignment are very important skills for accuracy. The middle area of the first pad of the index finger should rest comfortably on the trigger. Keep the front and rear sights aligned on the target. Acquire the sight picture. Slowly squeeze the trigger with the index finger until the gun fires. Arm, wrist, hand, thumb and other fingers do not move - they hold the gun steady.

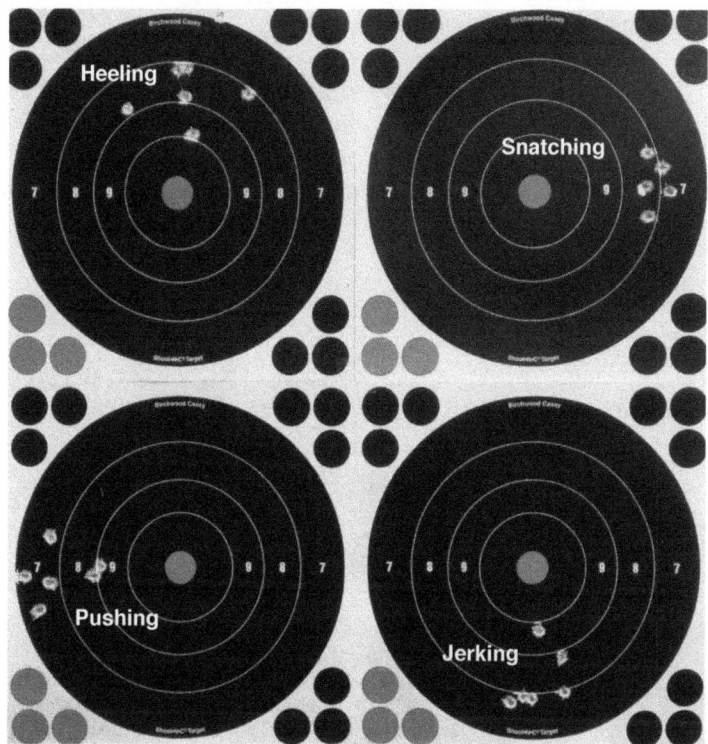

After taking several shots, take a break from shooting to study the hits on the target. These targets have four common errors made by beginning pistol shooters. Each error takes place at the instant the gun fires. These instructions concern analysis by right-handed shooters. For left-handed shooters, the 12 o'clock and 6 o'clock results are the same, but the 3 o'clock and 9 o'clock results must be reversed.

Heeling: Breaking the wrist upwards because of too much pressure from the heel of the hand to steady the gun, known as "heeling," pushes the shots upward to the 12 o'clock area of the target.

Snatching: Putting too much finger on the trigger, "known as snatching the trigger," is not squeezing straight back and so it pulls the muzzle to the right and sends the shots to the 3 o'clock area of the target.

Jerking: Anticipating the recoil, known as "jerking," causes the shots to go downward and hit low on the target in the 6 o'clock area.

Pushing: Too little finger on the trigger, less than the pad of the index finger, causes the shots to hit in the 9 o'clock area of the target. This trigger squeeze is not straight back and so pushes the muzzle to the left, known as "pushing."

If the handgun is too large or too small for the shooter's hand, it will be difficult to obtain a proper grip, including either too much or too little finger on the trigger. A bad grip and poorly executed trigger squeeze will cause inaccurate or inconsistent hits on the target. A proper trigger finger position is when the pad of the index finger reaches comfortably to rest on and squeeze the the trigger.

Seek Advice

Like any sport, handgun shooting accuracy gets better with practice, and practice improves with advice and training from pistol shooters who have greater experience.

On the shooting range at a sportsmen's club, pistol shooters help one another between courses of fire by offering advice to improve shooting skills. If a gun malfunctions or a cartridge misfires, other shooters will help resolve the problem. At competitive events, expert shooters may give advice to the novice to improve pistol shooting skills.

Obtain formal training from a certified instructor for refinement of pistol shooting skills. Gunsight Academy, founded by Lt. Col. Jeff Cooper in 1976, at www@gunsight.com is well known for its high quality courses, expert instructors and facilities. An Internet search will turn up other companies offering similar training.

Stay Up-To-Date

Membership in organizations that support firearms and the 2nd Amendment, such as the NRA, typically includes subscriptions to their magazines, including a focus on handguns. *American Rifleman* by the NRA is an example.

Publishers offer a variety of magazines that focus on handguns. Examples include: *American Handgunner*, *Guns and Ammo*, *Handguns* and *Shooting Times*.

The organizations, publishers and editors of these magazines frequently provide up-to-date information not only on the latest products, but also on federal and state laws pertaining to handgun ownership and use.

The handgun owner should make an effort to be well informed about all aspects of firearms.

Resources for Self-Help

In these times, the simplest way to obtain assistance on questions about handguns is by searching the Internet. The reader should have a critical eye to differentiate between accurate, high quality information and junk. Use the Internet, including pertinent YouTube videos, to develop knowledge and skills for safe and effective use of firearms and ammunition.

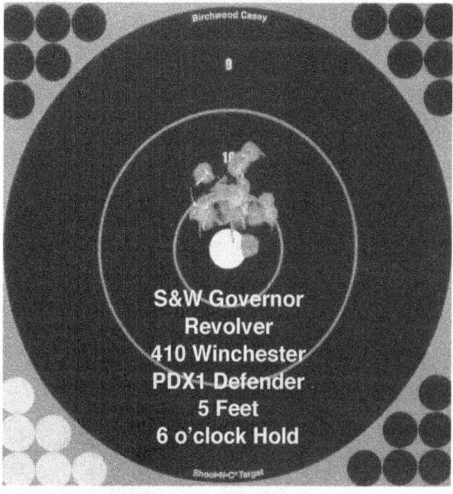

The choices and challenges for handgun shooting vary widely from practice at the shooting range with bulls eye targets or plinking at breakable objects, such as clay pigeons, to personal and home defense, to hunting small and big game, formal competitive events on state, regional and national levels, and the Olympic Games. How much to invest in the sport is up to the individual.

Pistol Shooting Styles and Competitions

NRA Action Pistol Shooting and Bianchi Cup

www.compete.nra.org

United States Practical Shooting Association

www.uspsa.org

International Defense Pistol Association

www.idpa.com

International Practical Shooting Confederation

www.ipsc.org

Steel Challenge Shooting Association

www.steelchallenge.com

Glock Shooting Sports Foundation

www.gssfonline.com

International Confederation of Revolver Enthusiasts

www.icore.org

The author posing with six outstanding graduates of his NRA Basic Pistol Class

Summary

The sporting activities associated with handgun ownership are varied, challenging and fun.

Safety is the constant watchword: the gun is always loaded; handle all guns safely by following the fundamental firearm safety rules - ACTT.

A beginning pistol shooter should obtain guidance from an instructor or experienced pistol shooter and practice shooting at bulls eye targets. This technique helps the beginner know quickly where the shots hit the target and how to analyze the target hits to improve accuracy. Success in every sport depends on regular and sustained practice. Handgun shooting proficiency benefits from practice.

There are many ways to stay up-to-date on handguns, including: membership in a sportsmen's club, membership in organizations that support firearms and the 2nd Amendment, subscription to handgun magazines, obtaining advanced levels of training, and consulting quality Internet-based sources for development of knowledge and skills.

Glossary

A

Accuracy - The ability to shoot a firearm repeatedly so that the projectiles consistently hit the center of the target in a small, tight cluster of shots.

Action - The assembly of moving parts of a firearm that loads, fires, ejects and reloads cartridges. The varieties of handgun actions for this discussion of revolvers and semi-automatic pistols are single action, double-action and double-action only. The discussion also identified the break-open action single shot handgun and the bolt action single shot handgun.

Ammunition - Guns fire ammunition, which for handguns consists of self-contained cartridges composed of a case, primer, powder and bullet.

B

Ballistics - The study of flight dynamics of projectiles - the movement of the bullet after a cartridge is fired in a gun. The three areas of ballistics are internal ballistics, external ballistics and terminal ballistics.

Barrel - A key feature of a firearm. The gun barrel is a metal tube through which the bullet travels when the cartridge is fired.

Barrel Compensator - A device at the muzzle-end of a gun barrel that vents gases from the fired cartridge just before the bullet exits the barrel on the way to the target. A barrel compensator helps prevent vertical movement of the barrel (or barrel flip). It assists with controlling the gun during firing, may reduce felt recoil and may improve accuracy. A barrel compensator tends to make the sound of the gun's firing much louder that it would be without the device.

Bench Rest - A bench at which a shooter sits and shoots to achieve maximum control of the handgun when taking shots at a target. Shooters may use sandbags, various gun mounts and vices for controlling the gun during firing.

Black Powder - A chemical compound consisting of specific portions of sulphur, charcoal and potassium nitrate (salt peter). The Chinese are generally recognized for the original development of black powder.

Bore - The inside of a gun barrel. A gun barrel is essentially a metal tube and the bore is the term for the inside of the barrel.

Bore Line - A straight line straight through the gun's bore to where the bullet would travel if not for the effects of gravity, which pulls the bullet downward as soon as it leaves the barrel. Gun sights correct the alignment of the gun with the target to compensate for gravity.

Brass - A slang term that applies to the empty cartridge case. The four parts of a pistol cartridge are: case, primer, powder and bullet.

Breath Control - The act of taking a deep breath, letting out a small portion of air and holding the breath for an instant to achieve greater control for an accurate shot with a gun.

Breech - The rear end of a gun barrel opposite the muzzle.

Bullet - The projectile fired from a gun. Bullets come in different sizes and shapes and are made of various materials and combinations of materials, including lead, copper, plastic and rubber.

Bullet Drop - As soon as the bullet leaves the muzzle after the cartridge fires, gravity pulls the bullet downward, causing the bullet's flight to be an arch, not a straight line as with the shooter's line of sight to the target. Air resistance and objects in the path of the bullet also affect its flight.

Bullet Jacket - An exterior coating of copper, brass or steel on the core of the bullet, which is typically made of lead.

Bulls Eye - The very center of a target.

C

Cabinet - A gun cabinet is a relatively low security system for storing firearms. Gun cabinets may be accessed with a key and may be made of wood or thin metal.

The gun safe is considered the most secure system for storing firearms when not in use.

Caliber - The measurement for the outside diameter of a bullet and the inside diameter - the bore - of a gun barrel. The gun's bore is measured from land to land. Caliber may be expressed in decimals (e.g., .22 caliber, .38 caliber and .45 caliber) or millimeters (e.g., 6.35 mm, 7.65 mm, and 9 mm).

Cartridge - The name for a single unit of ammunition. Self-contained cartridges, consisting of case, primer, powder and bullet are used in all modern firearms.

Case - The container, usually made of brass, aluminum or an alloy, that holds all other parts of a pistol cartridge, including primer, powder and bullet.

Cease Fire - A command that anyone present should shout out loud for all to hear in the event that the situation is unsafe at a shooting range or shooting event.

Centerfire - A type of cartridge that has the primer located in a tiny pocket in the center of the cartridge head.

Chamber - The place in the gun where the cartridge is stored until fired. A revolver will have several chambers to support repeat firing as the cylinder revolves; a semi-automatic pistol will have one chamber, which is the rear portion of the barrel opposite the muzzle, with additional cartridges stored in the magazine.

Cock - The act of setting the gun's action for taking the next shot, as in "cock the action." Also, the original term for the hammer of a muzzleloader firearm because its shape resembled the head of a rooster.

Cylinder - The device on a revolver for storing cartridges. A revolver cylinder will have several chambers for storage of cartridges to support repeat firing.

Cylinder Release Latch - A switch-like device on the side or top of the revolver. Operating the cylinder release latch allows the cylinder to swing out for loading, unloading, inspection and cleaning.

D

Discharge - The firing of a cartridge in a gun.

Double Action - A revolver or semi-automatic may be designed for double action firing, where a squeeze of the trigger completes two steps: cocks the firing mechanism and releases the hammer to fire the cartridge.

Double Action Only - Some revolvers and semi-automatic pistols are designed for double action only, where a squeeze of the trigger completes two steps: cocks the firing mechanism and releases the hammer to fire the cartridge. Squeezing the trigger on the double action only handgun requires a hard pull of 10 - 12 pounds, unlike single action, which can be as little as 2 pounds. A double action only handgun cannot function in the single action mode.

E

Eddie Eagle Program - The gun safety program from the National Rifle Association that is taught to children starting in first grade. It consists basically of four rules for children to follow: "If you see a gun: STOP! Don't Touch. Leave. Tell an Adult."

Ejection - The act of removing a cartridge from a gun's chamber.

Empty Chamber Indicator - A yellow or orange plastic flag with a long flexible tip sized for the bore of the gun that the shooter puts into the gun's open action and through the barrel when at a shooting range and not in the process of firing the gun. Also referred to as the "ECI."

Extraction - The process of a gun's action to remove a cartridge from the chamber.

F

Firearm - A gun that discharges a projectile. Commonly, firearms are understood to be a type of small arm or weapon that uses cartridges loaded with gunpowder as the propellant.

Firing - The act of shooting a gun.

Firing Line - The line, imaginary or painted, on a shooting range - often just behind a long shooters' bench with a number of shooting positions identified - where shooters assemble, lined up left to right, for target practice or competitive shooting events.

Firing Pin - A needle-shaped part that is struck by the hammer or internal firing mechanism. When the firing pin strikes the primer of a cartridge the live round detonates to fire the gun.

Flintlock - A primitive muzzleloader gun firing system that uses a piece of stone (flint). The gun's hammer grips a piece of flint. When the hammer is released, the flint strikes a steel frizzen, creating sparks that cause the priming powder to burn, which in turn causes the gunpowder charge in the barrel to burn.

Follow Through - Follow through is completing everything for the shot correctly: before the cartridge fires, when the cartridge fires and after the cartridge fires - including holding the correct sight picture. Developing good follow through is difficult, but when shots are consistently forming tight groups on the target, preferably in the X-ring, the shooter has acquired the skill.

Forcing Cone - The end of the gun barrel, the breech-end of the gun barrel, opposite the muzzle, that is designed to help guide the bullet into the rifling when the cartridge is fired.

Frame - A main part of a handgun that all other parts are attached to.

Full Cock - The position of the hammer when pulled all the way to the rear, locking the action in readiness for squeezing the trigger to fire the gun.

G

Grip - The handle of a handgun. The gun may be fired by holding the grip with one or both hands. Also, correct grip refers to the effective way a shooter holds the grip of the handgun to obtain consistently accurate hits on the target.

Grooves - Low points of rifling on the inside of a gun barrel. Rifling consists of spiraling cuts from the manufacturing process, with high points (lands) and low points (grooves) that impart a spin on the bullet as it passes through the barrel and continues on to the target.

Group - When several shots have been taken at a target, they may form a close collection of hits on the target. This is called a group. Achieving consistently tight groups on a target is the main goal of target practice and competitive shooting.

Gun - The original term for a firearm having a firing mechanism that discharges a projectile (from "gunne," meaning war machine).

H

Half Cock - On pre-modern guns and single action revolvers, this is the position of the hammer where it stops half way to full cock to facilitate loading. unloading and cleaning of the gun. Squeezing the trigger when the hammer is on half cock will not release the hammer to fire the cartridge.

Hammer - The hammer is the part on a firearm that resembles the common tool called a hammer. When the trigger is squeezed, the hammer is released to strike the firing pin and fire the cartridge. Not all handguns have exposed hammers and some handguns are hammerless, where the gun is fired by squeezing the trigger to release a spring-activated firing pin.

Handgun - A general term that is interchangeable with pistol. It is a firearm that has no stock, as found on a rifle or shotgun, and has a relatively short barrel. A handgun is designed to be handheld and fired by one or both hands.

Hangfire - A perceptible delay in the ignition of a cartridge after being struck by the firing pin, but the cartridge fires within 30 seconds.

Head - The closed end of a cartridge case, which may be stamped with identification about the cartridge caliber, load and manufacturer.

Headstamp - A mark pressed into the head of a cartridge case giving name of the cartridge manufacturer and the name and caliber of the cartridge.

Hits - The individual holes punched into a target by the bullets.

J

Jam - A gun's action may jam (malfunction) when there is an issue with the cartridge size, load, general condition or firing; or if the gun's action is dirty, lacks appropriate lubrication or has one or more defective parts.

K

Kick - A slang term for the recoil a shooter feels when a cartridge is fired in a gun.

L

Lands - High points of rifling on the inside of a gun barrel. Rifling consists of spiraling cuts from the manufacturing process, with high points (lands) and low points (grooves) that impart a spin on the bullet as it passes through the barrel and continues on to the target.

Line of Sight - A straight line that extends from the shooter's eye through the gun's sights to the bulls eye of the target. A bullet that is fired from a gun does not travel the line of sight, but due to the affects of gravity and the set up of the gun's sights, its trajectory is upward in an arc to strike the target.

Load - The amount of gunpowder included in a cartridge. A load of powder may be standard, +P or +P+, signifying varying levels of pressure from lower to higher that will develop when the cartridge is fired. The term "load" is also a range command for official shooting matches. At this command all shooters may load a cartridge into the chamber and close the gun's action in preparation for live fire.

M

Magazine - A storage device for cartridges in a semi-automatic firearm.

Misfire - When the firing pin strikes the cartridge, but the cartridge does not fire. To avoid an instance of a hangfire, which is a delay in cartridge ignition but the cartridge fires within a few seconds, the shooter must wait 30 seconds before determining what caused the misfire.

Muzzle - The end of the barrel that the bullet exits on its way to the target.

Muzzleloader - A gun that is loaded with powder and a bullet or shot pellets from the muzzle end of the barrel. Modern firearms, by comparison, use self-contained cartridges. In a muzzleloader firearm the gunpowder and bullets are loaded separately as individual parts from the muzzle-end. The primer is loaded last. Common muzzleloader priming systems in use today are percussion and flintlock.

P

Percussion - A muzzleloader gun firing system that relies on a percussion cap (a tiny metal cap containing an impact detonating chemical compound) as a primer to fire the gunpowder. When the hammer strikes the percussion cap, the primer creates sparks and heat to fire the powder charge in the barrel.

Pistol - A general and interchangeable term for a handgun. Also, pistol is used as a specific reference to any handgun with a semi-automatic action.

Plinking - Casual, informal practice with a handgun where solid objects, such as soft drink cans, melons or water-filled plastic bottles may be used as targets.

Plus-P Load - A cartridge loaded with an amount of powder above the standard load, designed to increase the pressure of the fired cartridge. Also signified as +P. Do not use +P loads in handguns designed for standard loads only.

Plus-P-Plus Load - A cartridge loaded with an amount of powder above the +P load, designed to increase the pressure of the fired cartridge. Also signified as +P+. Do not use +P+ loads in handguns designed for standard loads only.

Powder - A shortened word for gunpowder, which is the propellant loaded into a cartridge and when fired pushes the bullet through the barrel and on to the target.

Pressure - Pressure is produced by the burning gunpowder when a cartridge is fired, with the effect of pushing the bullet through the barrel and on its way to the target. Different varieties of gunpowder produce varying amounts of pressure to produce lower or higher bullet velocities.

Primer - An impact sensitive chemical compound that when struck by the firing pin creates sparks and heat to fire the powder in a cartridge.

Propellant - Gun powder that is loaded into a cartridge. When the gun powder is fired by the primer after it is struck by the firing pin, the propellant burns, creating pressure, heat and gasses that force the bullet through the barrel and on to the target.

R

Recoil - The kick that the shooter feels when a cartridge fires in a gun. Recoil is a rearward push of the gun at the instant the cartridge fires. How much recoil the shooter feels depends on the cartridge caliber and load the weight of the gun, the design of the gun's grip. A barrel compensator may reduce felt recoil. Because the grip is lower than the gun barrel, the recoil will result in a push to the rear and at the same time upward.

Reload - Reload is the act of putting loaded cartridges into a gun.

Revolver - A handgun with a cylinder, the gun's distinguishing characteristic, with separate chambers that are loaded with cartridges. Squeezing the trigger or pulling back the hammer to cock the action revolves the cylinder for repeat firing.

Ricochet - When a bullet strikes a hard surface, it bounces off, and the direction and length of travel are impossible to predict. A bullet ricochet is very dangerous. Never shoot at solid objects. Exceptions are official shooting matches where courses of fire may use materials, such as specially designed steel plates for use with various live fire activities that have been designed to prevent injury to shooters.

Rifling - Grooves cut on the inside of a gun barrel by the manufacturer that put a spin on the bullet as it passes through the barrel and travels to the target, increasing accuracy of the projectile.

Rimfire - A cartridge that has the primer compound located in the rim of the cartridge case. The centerfire cartridge has its primer in a small metal cap that is fitted into the center of the head of the cartridge case.

Round - A slang term for a cartridge. Also a term applied to another opportunity to shoot, as in "let's shoot another round."

S

Safe - A metal container for storing firearms and other valuables. Gun safes come in various sizes from small, accommodating only a few guns, to very large, for whole collections. Access to a gun safe may be a mechanical or electronic combination lock.

The gun safe is considered the most secure system for storing firearms when not in use.

Safety - A mechanical device activated by a lever or switch on the frame of a semi-automatic handgun. The purpose of the safety is to help prevent the unintended firing of the gun. Firearms may also have other safety mechanisms that are built into the action. Revolvers do not have external safety switches, but do have internal safety devices to prevent the firearm from discharging, especially when dropped. Similarly, some semi-automatic pistols do not have external safeties, but do have internal safeties.

A safety is a mechanical device that may fail to operate as intended.

Semi-Automatic - A firearm that has an action designed to fire, extract, and load cartridges automatically for repeat firing with each squeeze of the trigger. Often shortened to "semi-auto."

Shot - The act of firing a gun, called taking a "shot." Also a term applied to the lead pellets in a shotshell, such as the 410 shotshell featured in this book.

Sight Adjustment - The act of adjusting a gun sight system for accurate hits on a target. Adjustment of the rear sight with the open sight system requires moving the rear sight in the same direction as the hits should move on the target to obtain consistent hits in the X-ring. To adjust other sight systems, such as telescopic, holographic, red dot or laser sights, follow instructions from the manufacturer.

Sight Alignment - The act of aiming at a target with a gun, where the shooter correctly lines up the rear sight with the front sight and keeps both gun sights in alignment with the target.

Sights - Sights on a gun help a shooter aim at and hit a target accurately. Guns may have open, telescopic, red dot, laser or holographic sights, all of which serve the same basic purpose.

Single Action - A revolver or semi-automatic may be designed for single action shooting, where the hammer first must be cocked and then with the squeeze of the trigger, the hammer is released to fire the cartridge.

Slide - The distinguishing feature of semi-automatic handguns. When a cartridge fires in a semi-automatic pistol, pressure from the burning powder overcomes spring tension in the action, causing the slide to cycle rapidly to the rear and then forward to eject the spent cartridge case, load the next cartridge from the magazine and make the gun's action ready for repeat firing.

Slide Stays Back - On a semi-automatic pistol, when the last cartridge is fired, the gun's action keeps the slide locked to the rear. This condition of the pistol enables the quick removal of the empty magazine and replacement with a full magazine for repeat firing.

Squib Load - A cartridge that develops less-than-expected pressure when fired. A squib load may have no powder and only a primer, too little powder, contaminated powder or a defective primer. When fired, a squib load produces a low-level kick or recoil. Firing a squib load may create enough pressure to push the bullet into the barrel but not out of the barrel. A stuck bullet in a gun barrel must be removed manually before taking a followup shot because firing the next cartridge could explode the barrel, causing injury and possibly death to the shooter or bystanders.

Standard Load - An amount of powder in a cartridge that effectively discharges a bullet from the gun when fired. Higher loads of powder have these designations: +P and +P+ to signify a cartridge has a greater amount of powder than a standard load and also creates greater pressures when fired.

T

Target - The object a shooter aims at with a gun and wishes to hit with the bullet. Also, the target is whatever object the bullet strikes and where it comes to rest, which could be an object beyond the target and not the intended target. The shooter must always be sure of the target and what lies beyond the target.

Trajectory - The path of the bullet once it exits the barrel of the gun. Bullet trajectory is not a straight line to a target, as with eyesight, because gravity pulls the bullet downward as soon as it exits the muzzle causing the bullet's trajectory to be an arc. The Law of Gravity applies to the flight dynamics of all projectiles and is commonly experienced when playing sports involving movement of a ball as in golf, baseball, soccer and pingpong.

Trigger - A small lever, usually located inside the gun's trigger guard, that when squeezed to the rear of the firearm releases the firing pin to strike the primer of a cartridge and fire the gun.

Trigger Guard - A loop under the gun's frame inside of which is the trigger. The purpose of the trigger guard is to help prevent an unintended firing of the gun by accidentally touching the trigger.

Trigger Lock - A mechanical or electrical device that may be external to the firearm or built into the firearm's action and is designed to prevent access to or movement of the trigger to fire the gun.

Trigger Squeeze - The act of using the pad of the index finger (trigger finger) to pull back on the trigger in a smooth rearward motion to fire a gun.

V

Vault - A box-shaped gun security device, generally smaller than a safe, that has a mechanical, electrical or key access.

The gun safe is considered the most secure system for storing firearms when not in use.

W

Weapon - Any tool that might be used against another person or group of persons, but generally understood to be a gun or knife.

X

X-ring - The very center of a target.

Answers to Quiz Questions

Chapter 1

1. F, 2. A, 3 A

Chapter 2

1. B, 2. A, 3. B, 4. A, 5. A

Chapter 3

1. A, 2. A, 3. A, 4. B, 5. C. 6. A

Chapter 4

1. A, 2. A, 3. B, 4. B, 5. C, 6. B, 7. B, 8. D, 9. E, 10. A

Chapter 5

1. B, 2. A, 3. B, 4. A, 5. D, 6. A, 7. A, 8. B, 9. A

Chapter 6

1. A, 2. C, 3. B, 4. A, 5. A, 6. A, 7. A, 8. C9. A

Chapter 7

1. A, 2. B, 3. A, 4. A, 5. B, 6. B, 7. D, 8. B

Chapter 8

1, A, 2. A, 3. A, 4. A, 5. B, 6. B, 7. B, 8. A

Chapter 9

1. B, 2. A, 3. C, 4. A

Chapter 10

1. A, 2. C, 3. A

Chapter 11

1. B, 2. C, 3. D

Chapter 12

(no questions)

www.ingramcontent.com/pod-product-compliance
Lightning Source LLC
LaVergne TN
LVHW091306080426
835510LV00007B/385